MW00795690

"This book will help Anglicans around the world better understand and appreciate our Reformation heritage, its foundations in Holy Scripture, and its relevance for churches today. More than that, it will help us ground our worship, corporate or otherwise, in the gracious gospel of Jesus Christ."

Andrew Cheah, Dean, St Mary's Cathedral, Kuala Lumpur, Malaysia

"*Reformation Anglican Worship* is one of the most important books written in the last century and should be a prominent feature on every Anglican bookshelf. It abounds with quotable, concise, and meaningful insights that extend from Cyril of Alexandria to J. C. Ryle, giving the reader confidence to unravel the knotty problems that have intimidated many."

Henry L. Thompson III, Dean, President, and Associate Professor of Liturgical Studies, Trinity School for Ministry

"Liturgical worship has become the focus of much controversy as different provinces of the Anglican Communion have followed divergent paths. This book situates Anglican devotion in Holy Scripture and emphasizes the importance of both preaching and sacramental practice. A clarion call to a renewed way of thinking about these key subjects, it is faithful to the tradition without being hidebound to antiquarianism. Pastors, students, and liturgists will all benefit."

Gerald Bray, Research Professor of Divinity, History, and Doctrine, Beeson Divinity School

"This fresh expression of Anglican spirituality roots our lives and our worship in the Scriptures, reminding us that the biblical narrative is preeminent in forming our worshipful and lived responses to God's grace."

Todd Hunter, Bishop, The Diocese of Churches for the Sake of Others

"Michael Jensen offers a new generation of Anglicans a refreshing opportunity to investigate and appreciate the Book of Common Prayer and its biblical roots. Cranmer's liturgies enable the grace of the gospel to be heard and gratitude to be expressed with repentance, faith, dedication, service, and praise. Jensen happily combines biblical, theological, historical, and liturgical insights to reveal the ongoing potential of this Reformation standard for edifying churches and promoting God-honoring worship today."

David Peterson, Emeritus Faculty Member, Moore College

"A clear understanding of Cranmer's prayer book—its background, content, meaning, and purpose—is essential if we are to continue in harmony as Anglican Christians. My wish is that every Anglican bishop, clergy, and layperson would read this excellent book."

John W. Yates II, Founding Pastor, The Falls Church Anglican, Falls Church, Virginia

"Michael Jensen not only gives us the historical and theological understanding of worship but also applies the principles to Anglican worship today. This is an essential book for Anglicans and all who are interested in learning the roots of Reformation Anglican worship."

Samy Fawzy Shehata, Bishop Coadjutor, Diocese of Egypt

"Jensen emphasizes the priority of grace in Christian worship. Because we experience God's abundant grace in forgiveness and healing, we can respond to him with gratitude, both personally and corporately. This results in fresh grace received for living the Christian life. The centrality of God's word, preached and taught, is everywhere in this book, but the author does not neglect the sacraments as channels of grace and means of receiving Christ. Jensen has given us a stimulating book for considering afresh the issues raised during the English Reformation and their impact on corporate worship."

Michael Nazir-Ali, Director, Oxford Centre for Training, Research, Advocacy and Dialogue

"I am thrilled with this clear, concise statement of the Reformation Anglican view of worship in language that is generous and accessible. Michael Jensen makes it clear that the Anglican Reformers simply wanted the prayer book to be God-centered, Christ-centered, and Bible-centered. I hope and expect that this volume will receive a wide readership."

Grant LeMarquand, Professor of Mission and Emeritus Professor of Biblical Studies, Trinity School for Ministry; Former Bishop for the Horn of Africa

"Michael Jensen's contribution to the Reformation Anglicanism Essential Library brings into sharp focus the grace-filled gospel center of historic Anglican worship and makes a spirited case for the place and purpose of preaching, prayer, song, and sacrament in the contemporary Christian gathering."

Kanishka Raffel, Dean of Sydney, Australia

Reformation Anglican Worship

THE REFORMATION ANGLICANISM ESSENTIAL LIBRARY

Edited by Ashley Null and John W. Yates III

THE REFORMATION ANGLICANISM ESSENTIAL LIBRARY

VOLUME 4

REFORMATION ANGLICAN WORSHIP

Experiencing Grace, Expressing Gratitude

MICHAEL P. JENSEN

WHEATON, ILLINOIS

Library of Congress Cataloging-in-Publication Data

Names: Jensen, Michael P. (Michael Peter), 1970– author.
Title: Reformation Anglican worship : experiencing grace, expressing gratitude / Michael P. Jensen.
Description: Wheaton, Illinois : Crossway, 2021. | Series: The Reformation Anglicanism essential library ; volume 4 | Includes bibliographical references and index.
Identifiers: LCCN 2020038979 (print) | LCCN 2020038980 (ebook) | ISBN 9781433572975 (hardcover) | ISBN 9781433572982 (pdf) | ISBN 9781433572999 (mobipocket) | ISBN 9781433573002 (epub)
Subjects: LCSH: Public worship—Anglican Communion—History.
Classification: LCC BX5141 .J46 2021 (print) | LCC BX5141 (ebook) | DDC 264/.03009—dc23
LC record available at https://lccn.loc.gov/2020038979
LC ebook record available at https://lccn.loc.gov/2020038980

For my sons

Contents

Introduction

Yet because there is no remedy, but that of necessity there must be some rules: therefore certain rules are here set forth, which as they be few in number; so they be plain and easy to be understood. So yet here you have an order for prayer (as touching the reading of holy scripture) much agreeable to the mind and purpose of the old fathers, and a great deal more profitable and commodious, than that which of late was used.

It is more profitable, because here are left out many things, whereof some be untrue, some uncertain, some vain and superstitious: and is ordained nothing to be read, but the very pure word of God, the holy scriptures, or that which is evidently grounded upon the same; and that in such a language and order, as is most easy and plain for the understanding, both of the readers and hearers.

Thomas Cranmer, preface to the 1549 Book of Common Prayer[1]

Uncommon Anglican Worship

On February 20, 1547, the nine-year-old Edward VI was crowned in Westminster Abbey. His archbishop, Thomas Cranmer, is reputed to have charged him with these words: "Your majesty is God's

---

1. Quoted in Joseph Ketley, ed., *Two Liturgies . . . of Edward VI* (Cambridge: Parker Society, 1844), 18–19.

vicegerent, and Christ's vicar within your own dominions, and to see, with your predecessor Josiah, God truly worshiped, and idolatry destroyed; the tyranny of the bishops of Rome banished from your subjects, and images removed."[2]

What Cranmer wanted to see in a Reformed Church of England—which he would institute over the next half-decade, with the king's help—was nothing less than a revolution in worship. Cranmer could have used these words before Henry VIII, for under the old king the idolatry of the saints' shrines had ended as the shrines were torn down. But now Cranmer was free to give his words a clearly Protestant meaning by applying them to the Mass, something that Henry would never have allowed. The evangelical gospel was a severe condemnation of the practices of medieval Catholicism and the theology of worship that it implied. The need for new forms of worship was urgent because the stakes were so high in Cranmer's mind: if the people were going to worship God rightly, then the unbiblical, distracting, and frankly idolatrous practices of the previous era needed to be repudiated and replaced with preaching and praying as means of fostering belief. Nothing less than individual salvation was in the balance.

What ensued was a complete renovation in the idea of worship along the lines of the Reformation gospel. In evangelical terms, worship was not the people offering something to God so that he would bless them but a means of preaching the gospel itself. Worship meant God giving to the people, and not the other way around. Liturgy was to be focused not on the work of the people but on their reception of the benefits of salvation. First in 1549 and then again in 1552, Cranmer gave the English people a pattern of worship that enshrined the priority of God's grace and gave voice to the people's response of gratitude in words they could understand. In these two editions of the Book of Common Prayer, Cranmer ensured that the word of God would not be silent among

---

2. Henry Jenkyns, ed., *The Remains of Thomas Cranmer*, 4 vols. (Oxford: Oxford University Press, 1833), 2:119.

the people of God. He presented to people the true character of God, the almighty and everlasting God "whose property is always to have mercy," that they might worship him as he truly is.[3] And he ensured that the death of Christ for sin was at the center of an Anglican piety.

The forms of worship created by Cranmer have become for many Anglicans the distinctive mark of their church. For some people, to say "Anglican" or "not Anglican" means something about the form of worship that is being used in a particular congregation. And yet, some four and a half centuries after Cranmer, the reality is that the churches of the worldwide Anglican Communion are not as united in their habits of corporate worship as one might think. Happily, most, if not all, provinces have authorized significant revisions of the Book of Common Prayer, updating and translating the language as necessary.

Some liberty has been allowed—or taken—to experiment for the sake of reaching the lost, such that traditional forms of worship exist side by side with highly informal gatherings. As a matter of fact, Cranmer had already imagined a time when a diversity of forms of worship would be needed for cultural and evangelistic reasons. It is worth examining Article 34 at this point:

XXXIV. Of the Traditions of the Church.

It is not necessary that traditions and ceremonies be in all places one, or utterly like, for at all times they have been diverse, and may be changed according to the diversity of countries, times, and men's manners, so that nothing be ordained against God's Word. Whosoever through his private judgment, willingly and purposely doth openly break the traditions and ceremonies of the Church, which be not repugnant to the Word of God, and be ordained and approved by common authority, ought to be rebuked openly, (that others may fear to do the like) as he that offendeth against the common order of the Church, and hurteth

---

3. Ketley, *Two Liturgies*, 92, 278.

the authority of the Magistrate, and woundeth the consciences
of the weak brethren.

Every particular or national Church hath authority to or-
dain, change, and abolish, ceremonies or rites of the Church
ordained only by man's authority, so that all things be done
to edifying.[4]

The principles for instituting ceremonies and rites for each new
era and place take into account "the diversity of countries, times,
and men's manners," so long as what is ordained by each church
is "done to edifying" and is not simply a matter of the exercise of
whim. The test is whether a particular form agrees with God's
word or not, and whether the principle of order is upheld or upset
by what is done as churches gather. In other words, there was, to
the Reformers' way of thinking about it, a need for flexibility and
even pragmatism about forms of worship—so long as the theological
principles were not cast aside, and as long as any new form served
the mission of the church to proclaim the gospel.

This is a matter of much greater concern in the churches of
the Anglican Communion today. The current diversity of forms
of worship represents not simply the practical needs of the gospel in each place but frequently a different theology of worship
altogether. Without knowledge of the theological principles of
Anglican worship, we are simply not able to discriminate between forms of worship that cloud or even dishonor God and
forms of worship that proclaim his truth. Instead, we simply do
what is right in our own eyes. In their various ways, the Anglo-
Catholic movement, the charismatic movement, and Reformed
evangelicals have pursued their own *theological* convictions about
Christian worship above and beyond the words on the pages of the
prayer book and into territory highly disputed by the other groups
within Anglicanism. What are we to make of this diversity, and
how can we evaluate it?

---

4. Charles Hardwick, *A History of the Articles of Religion* (Cambridge: Deighton Bell,
1859), 319 (all quotations from this source have modernized spelling).

If the stakes are as high as Cranmer set them in his charge to the young king, this cannot be a matter of simple indifference. That does not mean that intolerance and inflexibility ought to be the aim. But it does mean that we need to recollect what Cranmer and the other Reformers were trying to do when they prepared the Book of Common Prayer and commanded its use in the churches. Furthermore, it does mean that we need to seek out once more a proper scriptural and theological account of worship so that "nothing be ordained against God's Word."

That is the principle task of what follows in the book before you. My objective is to uncover the roots of the Reformation theology and practice of worship. But I am doing this not because I think it is simply a matter of historical interest. Nor am I interested in playing that old Anglican game—namely, the search for the allegedly most authentic reset point for Anglicanism—or to establish such a thing as "Anglican identity," which would be by extension a kind of imperial claim over other accounts of Anglican identity. While it is obviously my conviction that the theological commitments of Cranmer and the other English Reformers had, and still have, seminal significance for Anglicans and that the theology of this period has often been disregarded in a more than cavalier fashion (historical pun intended!), I am more interested in whether these theological convictions continue to be sound ones for today. That, it seems to me, is truest to the spirit of the Reformers, and indeed to orthodox Christian faith—that nothing be "repugnant to the Word of God."

That was crucial for Cranmer as a liturgist. He was a genuinely *theological* liturgist, seeking to enshrine a particular gospel by means of his revision of English worship. If vagueness or ambiguity is a feature of the Book of Common Prayer, such that different parties have simultaneously claimed to find their own theological convictions expressed therein, then that is not Cranmer's intention. Cranmer was clear about what he was repudiating, as his charge to King Edward demonstrates. He also clearly was

intending the Book of Common Prayer, the Articles of Religion
(in his time, forty-two), and the Book of Homilies to be a comple-
mentary set, mutually informing one another. The origins of the
distinctive Anglican worship—for which it is best known—lie in a
clear step away from the worship of the medieval Catholic Church
and the theological convictions that it represented. As Howe and
Pascoe write:

> If any Anglican prayer book is read in the light of the Articles,
> the thoroughly unique and Protestant nature of Anglicanism be-
> comes obvious. Without this interpretative framework, prayer
> books can be seen as deliberately ambiguous at times. This is
> part of the genius of Anglican worship. Elizabeth made certain
> that the sharp lines drawn in the area of doctrine were blurred
> in the area of worship to accommodate as many people as pos-
> sible. Sadly, in our day, the widespread neglect of the Articles
> has permitted such a diversity in the interpretation of the same
> liturgy that the worldwide Anglican Church has been thrown
> into much unnecessary and destructive confusion.[5]

In relatively recent times, the Latin slogan *lex orandi, lex cre-
dendi* (literally "the law of prayer is the law of belief," but usually
understood as "praying shapes believing" or "praying determines
belief") has been used to suggest that doctrine is subordinate to liturgy. Hence, *The Book of Alternative Services of the Anglican Church
of Canada* (1985) says:

> It is precisely the intimate relationship of gospel, liturgy, and
> service that stands behind the theological principle *lex orandi:
> lex credendi*, i.e., the law of prayer is the law of belief. This prin-
> ciple, particularly treasured by Anglicans, means that theology
> as the statement of the Church's belief is drawn from the liturgy,
> i.e., from the point at which the gospel and the challenge of
> Christian life meet in prayer. The development of theology is

---

5. John W. Howe and Samuel C. Pascoe, *Our Anglican Heritage: Can an Ancient Church Be
a Church of the Future?*, 2nd ed. (Eugene, OR: Cascade, 2010), loc. 780 of 4959, Kindle.

not a legislative process which is imposed on liturgy; liturgy is
a reflective process in which theology may be discovered.[6]

A number of things ought to be said about this principle, not
least that its alleged origins in the ancient church are certainly ques-
tionable. It was introduced into Anglicanism in the twentieth century, having been coined in the late nineteenth century by a French
Roman Catholic monk named Prosper Gueranger (1805–1875). But
even so, the principle is usually taken to mean (as it is in *The Book of
Alternative Services*) that doctrine is derived from worship, and not
the other way around; and that, as a result, theology is a groping to
describe the inexpressible experience of worship: it is "a reflective
process in which theology may be discovered." That is both a mis-
translation of the Latin and a poor description of the Reformation
Anglicanism of Thomas Cranmer. The Latin phrase is of course
reversible, such that "the law of belief is the law of prayer." Cranmer
was clearly in possession of a set of theological convictions that he
hoped to express through his liturgy. He knew what he was—and
wasn't—inviting English churchgoers to believe as they worshiped.
After all, the first major liturgical change that Cranmer instituted
under Edward VI had been the preaching of the doctrinal homilies
in the middle of the Latin Mass.

Perhaps this might be thought a somewhat distastefully com-
bative start to the book. Don't we live a world away from those old
controversies? Do we twenty-first-century Anglicans not recoil
from the violent outcomes of the disagreements of the sixteenth
century? Certainly we do. But this does not excuse the theological
fuzziness that besets contemporary Anglicanism. I would regard
the liturgical confusion of our present time as a distinct echo of
the controversies of the sixteenth century. Different *styles* of worship amount to nothing at all, as Cranmer knew. In which case, let
as many liturgical flowers bloom as can be planted. But a different

---

6. *The Book of Alternative Services of the Anglican Church of Canada* (Toronto: Anglican
Book Centre, 1985), 10.

theology of worship is indicative of a different view of how people come to know God—how they get saved and how they live before him, in other words. That is something worth caring about if we are to be authentically Christian.

In this book, therefore, I will be less concerned to outline my preferences for a particular style of church meeting than to explore the theological convictions that made the Anglicanism of the Reformation what it was and is today—and what it could be in the future.

What Is Worship?

But what is *worship*, in any case? At one level, people are generally sure that this English word means "what goes on in a church meeting." We ask, "Where do you worship," and expect the answer to be something like "St Botolph's, at 10 a.m." A more specific usage equates congregational singing with worship, such that there are "worship pastors" and "worship leaders" (who are usually musicians) and "worship albums." These uses of the word reflect its dictionary definitions, which describe worship as the reverence offered to a divine power and the acts in which such reverence is expressed.[7]

But these common uses of the word *worship* are slightly misleading. For one thing, it is certainly the case that worship can be carried out by individuals who are not participating in a meeting in a church building. A believer can feed on Christ through his word, as Cranmer puts it, at any time or place.[8] For another, what constitutes an act or an expression of worship is actually broader than the common usage indicates. Both Testaments of the Bible push the people of God to regard worship not simply as religious activity but as a form of life. The Old Testament in particular is vigorous in its condemnation of false worship and worship corrupted by evil behavior.

---

7. The *Concise Oxford Dictionary* defines *worship* as "homage or reverence paid to a deity, esp. in a formal service." A secondary meaning is "adoration or devotion comparable to religious homage shown towards a person or principle," as in "the worship of wealth." *Concise Oxford Dictionary*, ed. R. E. Allen (Oxford: Oxford University Press, 1990), 1414.

8. Jenkyns, *Remains of Cranmer*, 3:319–20.

This is a point on which the English Reformers would absolutely insist in their theological thinking about worship.

It may also be dangerously misleading if, by using the word *worship*, we imply (even accidently) that it is by our offerings of worship that we make ourselves acceptable to God. The Reformation insight was that this notion of worship was based on a horrifying self-delusion; for fallen human beings are, on their own merits, incapable of giving true worship to the one being who is worthy of that adoration. True worship is, in fact, opened up for Christian believers only by Jesus Christ's worship of the Father. For Christians, then, worship engages with God only as a response to the prior grace he shows us in Jesus Christ.

Nevertheless, as you can see from the table of contents of this book, I have accepted the common definition of *worship* as indicating what Christian believers do when they gather. The important thing for us, as it was for Cranmer, is whether or not this activity known as worship is understood biblically. I will be asking, if the Reformation formularies of the Church of England, along with the intentions of the evangelical Reformers, are taken seriously, then what do we learn about the biblical theology and practice of the gathered worship of the congregation? But I will be seeking to place this concept of corporate worship within the wider sense of worship that a properly Christian theology of worship demands.

The first two chapters of this book are an exposition of the Reformation Anglican understanding of worship, which of course stems from the Reformation Anglican understanding of the gospel of Jesus Christ. The insistence of the Reformers on new forms of worship was not incidental or simply an updating of what had gone before. It represented a transformation of the previous habits of worship in light of a recovered theological understanding of salvation itself. For the English Reformers in Henrician and Edwardian England, human sin was far more intractable, and God's grace far more extraordinary, than they had previously understood it to be. They wanted people to know and express this as they worshiped.

Salvation was no longer thought to be mediated through the sacraments and servants of the church but was through the gospel of the crucified Christ revealed in the pages of Scripture.

That commitment to the authoritative voice of the Bible gives shape to this book. Thus, in chapter 1, I seek to lay out the kind of theology of worship that undergirded the Reformation by starting with Scripture itself. Since my purpose here is not simply antiquarian, it is vital to revisit the biblical sources of evangelical worship. Chapter 2 is an account of that journey in the sixteenth century, beginning with Thomas Cranmer and his prayer books. I will show that the theology—and yes, what we might call the "spirituality," or the "piety"—of receiving grace with gratitude is the basis for a distinctive approach to worship. There is, as Charles Hefling has written, "not much question where on the larger theological map the book [Book of Common Prayer] belongs. It was put there by its principal writer, Archbishop Thomas Cranmer, who deliberately fashioned the prayer book services so as to take one side rather than another in the theological controversies of his day."[9]

The opening two chapters are then expanded as I investigate the various activities of the gathered church and how they spring from, or ought to spring from, an evangelical account of worship. We begin, in chapter 3, with preaching and the word, noting that Cranmer enshrined a very prominent place for the preaching and reading of Scripture in the vernacular in the English church. This was a result of his central theological conviction that, as Paul says, "faith comes from hearing" (Rom. 10:17). For Cranmer, the written word of God was the instrument by which believers were *told*, *turned*, and *tethered* (as Ashley Null explains).[10]

Chapter 4 addresses itself to the controversial matter of the sacraments. Without question, the sacraments had a cherished place

9. Charles C. Hefling, "Introduction: Anglicans and Common Prayer," in *The Oxford Guide to the Book of Common Prayer: A Worldwide Survey*, ed. Charles C. Hefling and Cynthia L. Shattuck (Oxford: Oxford University Press, 2006), 3.

10. Dr. Null commonly uses these verbal adjectives about Cranmer's understanding of Scripture when he gives lectures to churches.

within the theology of Reformation Anglicanism while providing the focus for some of its most deadly disagreements, even among the Reformers. The meaning and nature of baptism and the Lord's Supper have been contested by Anglicans ever since. However, the Reformation formularies (like Cranmer himself) were quite clear about what the sacraments were not. A Reformation Anglican view of the sacraments is distinctly Reformed without lapsing into mere memorialism. The chapter then addresses the place of the sacraments for Reformation Anglicanism today.

In the fifth chapter, I address the subject of prayer. That Cranmer called his book the Book of Common Prayer and not the Book of Common Worship should not escape our notice. The very structure of the prayers written for the prayer book and for its successors frames the congregation in its relationship to God. More recent liturgies have not simply modernized the language of prayer but frequently changed the nature of our address to God—which is as serious a theological development as can be imagined. A change in the names for God can in fact reveal a change in the identity of God—by which we may again note that a completely different doctrine of God is at play.

Lastly, in chapter 6, I discuss the place and purpose of music in worship and as worship. Corporate worship within Christianity is always marked by singing. Today, of course, there are massive controversies over the role and place of music, and the charismatic movement has led to a new emphasis on contemporary and more popular forms of music. There were no less intense discussions about the place of music in the sixteenth century, with the cathedral choirs surviving the attempts of more radical elements to dismantle them. The arguments about musical style are a distraction from the principles outlined in the Reformation, in which the word of God must be served by musical forms and not made subservient to it. The chapter contains a challenge to churches everywhere to make use of music in line with these principles.

The Reformers of the sixteenth century were convinced that the right pattern of corporate worship was essential for the spiritual health of the people of God, and even for the evangelization of the nation. We need not imagine that anything has changed on that score. My prayer is that the churches that share an Anglican heritage might be led by those who have considered carefully the theological convictions of that heritage in the light of Scripture, those who lead God's people in the exclusive and fervent worship of the Father in the name of Jesus Christ and in the power of the Holy Spirit. May this book be of use in achieving that glorious end.

CHAPTER 1

The Heart of Christian Worship

... the Church being both a society and a society supernatural, although as it is a society it have the selfsame original grounds which other politic societies
have, namely, the natural inclination which all men
have unto sociable life, and consent to some certain
bond of association, which bond is the law that ap-
pointeth what kind of order they shall be associated
in: yet unto the Church as it is a society supernatural
this is peculiar, that part of the bond of their association which belong to the Church of God, must be a law
supernatural, which God himself hath revealed concerning that kind of worship which his people shall do
unto him. The substance of the service of God therefore, so far-forth as it hath in it anything more than
the law of reason doth teach, may not be invented of
men, as it is amongst the Heathens, but must be received from God himself, as always it hath been in
the Church, saving only when the Church hath been
forgetful of her duty.

Richard Hooker, *Of the Laws of Ecclesiastical Polity*[1]

---

1. Richard Hooker, *Of the Laws of Ecclesiastical Polity*, ed. Arthur Stephen McGrade (Cambridge: Cambridge University Press, 1989), 118 (1.15.2).

In chapter 2, I will sketch out the formation of a distinctively Reformed pattern of worship in sixteenth-century England. However, this pattern was not pulled out of thin air. It was derived from a rereading, in the original languages, of the true source of Christian faith: the Holy Scriptures. Hence, my first task is to outline in this chapter a biblical and theological rationale for Christian worship. Biblical faith is not, as we shall see, romantic about the human religious spirit. On the contrary, human beings face something of a crisis of worship. On the one hand, we are made for worship, but, on the other, we are predisposed to worship gods of our own making. In the Old Testament, we are taught that the holy God demands exclusivity in worship. He commands how his name should be honored and provides the means by which he can be rightly worshiped. But the tragic history of Israel prepares the field for the appearance of the one who will, on behalf of all humankind, truly worship: Jesus Christ, Son of David by lineage and declared "Son of God" by the Spirit. Christian worship therefore needs to be understood in the light of Jesus's worship. That necessarily leads us to think about Christian worship in the light of the doctrine of the Trinity—not simply that it is worship of the triune God but also that worship of the triune God has a distinct shape which is a critique of alternative forms of worship. This Trinitarian worship, as we shall see, has implications for Christian mission and for a Christian view of politics.

The Problem of Worship

If *worship* is the English term we use to describe the ways in which human beings seek to engage with God,[2] then one rather disturbing feature of the Old Testament witness is its blistering attacks on some worship and worshipers. There is no hallowing of the human religious spirit. False or corrupt or heartless worship is as great an evil as the Old Testament writers can imagine. Listen to Deuteronomy 29:16–20:

---

2. This is David Peterson's phrase in *Engaging with God: A Biblical Theology of Worship* (Leicester: Apollos, 1992), 20.

You know how we lived in the land of Egypt, and how we came through the midst of the nations through which you passed. And you have seen their detestable things, their idols of wood and stone, of silver and gold, which were among them. Beware lest there be among you a man or woman or clan or tribe whose heart is turning away today from the LORD our God to go and serve the gods of those nations. Beware lest there be among you a root bearing poisonous and bitter fruit, one who, when he hears the words of this sworn covenant, blesses himself in his heart, saying, "I shall be safe, though I walk in the stubbornness of my heart." This will lead to the sweeping away of moist and dry alike. The LORD will not be willing to forgive him, but rather the anger of the LORD and his jealousy will smoke against that man, and the curses written in this book will settle upon him, and the LORD will blot out his name from under heaven.

Secular and biblical anthropologies seem to agree that human beings are predisposed to worship.[3] They are by orientation likely to seek a transcendent other or others to whom to express adoration. If we are to believe some paleoanthropologists, even the Neanderthals had some form of religious practices. From the biblical perspective, the story of the original couple in Eden depicts them as walking in the state of complete communion with God for which they were created. Their terrible lapse resulted in the permanent compromise of that fellowship with God but did not remove their desire for it. From the point of view of the Old Testament Wisdom Literature, "He has made everything beautiful in its time. Also, he has put eternity into man's heart, yet so that he cannot find out what God has done from the beginning to the end" (Eccles. 3:11). Most poignantly, Paul outlines the human predicament in Romans 1:20–21:

For his invisible attributes, namely, his eternal power and divine nature, have been clearly perceived, ever since the creation of the world, in the things that have been made. So they are

---

3. The greatest study in this field is surely William James, *The Varieties of Religious Experience: A Study in Human Nature* (1902; repr., New York: Modern Library, 1994).

without excuse. For although they knew God, they did not honor him as God or give thanks to him, but they became futile in their thinking, and their foolish hearts were darkened.

Paul, who observed the blind religiosity of the Athenians in Acts 17, here explains that there is a kind of suppressed natural knowledge of God given to humankind. It amounts to a willful unknowing, a refusal to acknowledge what instinctively they know to be the case. Human beings are persistently religious; they seek to worship whenever they can.

Yet, according to the Old Testament, *it is possible to worship a false god.* "The nations" give devotion to gods like Baal or Asherah or Dagon—gods who did not create the heavens and the earth and are not worthy of worship. The famous challenge between Elijah and the priests of Baal on Mount Carmel, recorded in 1 Kings 18, is a pointed satire against the worship of a false god. The prophets of Baal dance and sing and even cut themselves in order to get the attention of Baal, but to no avail. Likewise, the statue of the Philistine deity Dagon falls flat on its face in a gesture of worship before the ark of the covenant in 1 Samuel 5. Worship of these deities is not simply wrong. It is foolish, since they are so obviously powerless.

In particular, the Old Testament reserves its greatest hostility for the practice of idolatry. Idol worship is ludicrous because the idol is impotent. In Isaiah 40–66, among the great declarations of the saving intentions of YHWH,[4] we read a fierce indictment of the practice of idolatry:

> To whom then will you liken God,
> or what likeness compare with him?

---

4. Y-H-W-H are the four Hebrew consonants in the personal name of the God of the Israelites and therefore properly known as the tetragrammaton (Greek for "having four letters"). Hebrew scribes thought this personal name too sacred to be pronounced by humans, so they wrote the vowels from the Hebrew word *Adonai* (my Lord) or *Elohim* (God) with the four consonants as a reminder that another word should be said instead of the personal name of God. The combination of YHWH with these vowels eventually lead the translators of the King James Bible to render the tetragrammaton as "Jehovah." Modern Bibles usually translate the tetragrammaton as either "Lord" (with large and small capitals to distinguish it from the Hebrew word for "Lord") or "Yahweh" (which uses what scholars believe were the original vowels for the tetragrammaton).

An idol! A craftsman casts it,
>	and a goldsmith overlays it with gold
>	and casts for it silver chains.
He who is too impoverished for an offering
>	chooses wood that will not rot;
he seeks out a skillful craftsman
>	to set up an idol that will not move. (Isa. 40:18–20)

In Isaiah 44, there is an extended passage in which the author heaps ridicule on those who would make an idol with their own human hands and then in some way consider it divine. "All who fashion idols are nothing, and the things they delight in do not profit. Their witnesses neither see nor know, that they may be put to shame. Who fashions a god or casts an idol that is profitable for nothing?" (Isa. 44:9–10). The idol can do no good: it is simply dumb. Why would anyone do this? And yet, the habit is ingrained in human behavior. The idol-maker does not even seem to realize that the profane use he makes of the wood left over from his idol manufacture reveals the idiocy of his practice.

> Half of it he burns in the fire. Over the half he eats meat; he roasts it and is satisfied. Also he warms himself and says, "Aha, I am warm, I have seen the fire!" And the rest of it he makes into a god, his idol, and falls down to it and worships it. He prays to it and says, "Deliver me, for you are my god!" (Isa. 44:16–17)

Israel itself is not guiltless of this kind of worship. The most famous incident is, of course, the episode of the golden calf: "And [Aaron] received the gold from their hand and fashioned it with a graving tool and made a golden calf. And they said, 'These are your gods, O Israel, who brought you up out of the land of Egypt!'" (Ex. 32:4). It is an absurd claim, and terrible consequences quickly unfold. The Old Testament is by no means syncretistic.

If it is possible to worship an entirely false god, *it is also possible to worship the true God falsely.* YHWH does not merely forbid worship of other gods. He also demands that he be worshiped as he directs. He must be approached on his terms, rather than through the whims of human beings. In the description of the tabernacle cult with its elaborate construction and its provision for sacrifice in Exodus 25, there is no doubt that the direction for its creation comes from YHWH and not from the imaginations of the people. It is the provision for a visible means of engagement with an invisible Deity who, at the same time, does not compromise his invisibility or reduce his splendor.

The episode of Balaam in Numbers 23–24 is illustrative of a false worshiper of the true God. The non-Israelite Balaam recognizes YHWH but does not recognize or give due honor to his people. In 1 Samuel 13, Saul is condemned for his self-legislation with regard to sacrifices to YHWH. The mistreatment of the ark of the covenant in 1 Samuel 5–7—an attempt to use it as a talisman in battle—shows that simply identifying the true God is not sufficient to worship him rightly, for Israel clearly does not understand who YHWH is, even if they can name him. But the supreme example of this error is in the garden, where Adam and Eve do not seek to worship some other god but rather disobey the true God's command.

These two forms of false worship were frequently combined in Israel's history as they mixed worship of the nations' pagan deities with worship of YHWH. This was Solomon's great flaw—he allowed the gods of his many wives to turn his heart (see 1 Kings 11:3), and he built shrines to them alongside the extraordinary temple that made his name.

> For Solomon went after Ashtoreth the goddess of the Sidonians, and after Milcom the abomination of the Ammonites. So Solomon did what was evil in the sight of the LORD and did not wholly follow the LORD, as David his father had done. Then Solomon built a high place for Chemosh the abomination of Moab, and for Molech the abomination of the Ammonites, on the mountain east of Jerusalem. And so he did for all his foreign wives, who made offerings and sacrificed to their gods. (1 Kings 11:5–8)

The prophets expressed their shock at Israel's and Judah's readiness to engage with a smorgasbord of gods in clear disobedience of YHWH, to whom they owed their very existence. They explained the historical disaster of the Babylonian exile as a divine judgment on the syncretism of the people of God. For example:

> I will stretch out my hand against Judah
>   and against all the inhabitants of Jerusalem;
> and I will cut off from this place the remnant of Baal
>   and the name of the idolatrous priests along with the priests,
> those who bow down on the roofs
>   to the host of the heavens,
> those who bow down and swear to the LORD
>   and yet swear by Milcom. (Zeph. 1:4–5)

The divine jealousy (*qin'ah*) is the lesson to be relearned from Zephaniah. An apparently sophisticated blend of worship practices and deities is, more than any other human activity, destined to provoke the ire of the God of the Bible.

However, a third form of worship is also subject to critique in the Old Testament. *It is possible to worship the true God truly but have that worship rendered null by corrupt behavior.* The rituals and observances of the temple, with its elaborate sacrifices and festivals, might all be performed in true order. But if the hearts of the people are not rightly tuned, then the outward observance of the cult is meaningless. The prophecy recorded in Ezekiel 34 against the "shepherds of Israel" critiques them for their exploitation of the people. Micah's thunderous revelation against the people focuses on the evil behavior of their leaders rather than their irreligion:

> Hear, you heads of Jacob
>   and rulers of the house of Israel!
> Is it not for you to know justice?—
>   you who hate the good and love the evil,
> who tear the skin from off my people
>   and their flesh from off their bones,

> who eat the flesh of my people,
>> and flay their skin from off them,
> and break their bones in pieces
>> and chop them up like meat in a pot,
>> like flesh in a cauldron.
>
> Then they will cry to the LORD,
>> but he will not answer them;
> he will hide his face from them at that time,
>> because they have made their deeds evil. (Mic. 3:1–4)

The punishment for the evil behavior is that the Lord will make himself absent—their worship, however earnest and accurate, will be rendered empty.

In Psalm 51, David's famous psalm of confession, he notes that it is possible to worship the true God in the directed way but without reality on account of a moral failing. He writes:

> For you will not delight in sacrifice, or I would give it;
>> you will not be pleased with a burnt offering.
> The sacrifices of God are a broken spirit;
>> a broken and contrite heart, O God, you will not despise.
>> (Ps. 51:16–17)

Sacrifice has no effect in the context of David's abuse of his power, his adultery, and his murder of the faithful Uriah the Hittite.

We shall turn to the New Testament's theology of worship in due course; suffice it to say here that the Old Testament critique of false worship is the significant backdrop against which Jesus's identity must be established. How is worship of him not false worship? How does the Hebrew theology of worship mesh with what follows in the New Testament if the two are not to be understood as substantially opposed to one another?

But the critique of false worship offered in the Old Testament is also a significant pointer to what true worship must be if it is to be worship of the true God. Worship is not simply good in and of itself.

It cannot be simply the invention of human beings. It cannot be a description of a human movement toward God. It cannot be shared or blended across a portfolio of deities. It cannot be a desperate plea for God's attention from the human side. It cannot presume, by its own devices, to overturn the divine judgment that stands against us in our fallen state.

Engaging with God on God's Terms

What the attacks on false worship reveal is that, in biblical terms at least, worship of the God of Israel is exclusively on his terms. As the Anglican scholar David Peterson says in his magisterial work *Engaging with God: A Biblical Theology of Worship*, "Worship of the living and true God is essentially an engagement with him on the terms that he proposes and in the way that he alone makes possible."[5] This is not simply an observation about the demands of the jealous God; it is also a statement about the human condition. True worship is not possible unless God himself enables it, because human beings are unable to truly worship him without his enabling.

If we are to understand it in biblical terms, the English word *worship* names what the people of God do in *response* to the divine initiative. Peterson explains how divine initiative leads to human response:

> Acceptable worship in Old Testament terms involves homage, service and reverence, demonstrated in the whole of life. A common factor in these three ways of describing Israel's response to God is the assumption that he had acted towards them in revelation and redemption, to make it possible for them to engage with him acceptably.[6]

YHWH is the God who reveals himself to his people and, in revealing himself, redeems them. In redeeming them, he enables them to relate to him—something that was not previously possible.

---

5. Peterson, *Engaging with God*, 20.
6. Peterson, *Engaging with God*, 73.

God initiates a relationship with Abraham almost out of the blue, as it were, calling him to leave his homeland on the basis of the great threefold promise: a great nation, in a great place, with a great blessing. The trajectory of this promise is, from the outset, global, for "in you all the families of the earth shall be blessed" (Gen. 12:3). This God reveals himself to be a covenant-making God—a deity seeking an ongoing relationship with humanity. The word of God comes to Abraham in the midst of many things that contradict it (including his great age), so that it is a struggle for him to believe it. And yet, this word is not simply about the present but about the future that God will bring to pass. Abraham and his descendants are taught the theological lesson that God is the God who creates and redeems out of nothing; and thus they depend on him absolutely.

The Abraham narrative is the prelude for the main movement, which is the encounter of the people of Israel with God in the exodus. In that event, YHWH both reveals his name and redeems his people—his acts of redemption and revelation are intertwined with one another. Under the leadership of the aged Moses, he brings them to the "mountain of God," Mount Sinai. At Sinai, God tells Moses:

> Thus you shall say to the house of Jacob, and tell the people of Israel: "You yourselves have seen what I did to the Egyptians, and how I bore you on eagles' wings and brought you to myself. Now therefore, if you will indeed obey my voice and keep my covenant, you shall be my treasured possession among all peoples, for all the earth is mine; and you shall be to me a kingdom of priests and a holy nation." These are the words that you shall speak to the people of Israel. (Ex. 19:3–6)

The Israelites are the witnesses of God's mighty act in defeating the Egyptians and of its extraordinary consequence: "I . . . brought you to myself." What then follows is a description of the ongoing terms of the relationship with YHWH, along with all its stipulations and patterns. God himself lays out for the people the context for an acceptable response of worship to the almighty God—a pattern of life that distinguishes them as his but begins with their acknowledging him as Lord and Redeemer. At Sinai, God makes himself known to Israel and, in doing so, reveals his intention to be a special presence among them. They are to be known as the people among whom God himself dwells. His special character of holiness is to become a character that they share and to which they give expression in their manner of life.

They are to be "a kingdom of priests and a holy nation." This signifies that the whole of Israel's existence will be shaped by this relationship with YHWH. This will not be an occasional matter of observance. It is to be a distinctive, identifying mark of this people. They are in this way to be separated from the nations that surround them. But the notion of priesthood is significant here if we recall that the promise to Abraham was for the blessing of all the families on the earth. The Israelites were to be the people who demonstrated to all peoples what it was like to belong to YHWH, the Lord of heaven and earth. His character was to be embodied in their community life.

This then is the background to the giving of the Torah, or "the law." The law was neither simply moral nor simply ritual. Both dimensions of the law were outlined as a matter of delimiting the boundaries for life together with God. Note that there was no sense of opposition between the notion of a divinely given word and the indescribable majesty and holiness of God's character. As at the mountain, so in the tabernacle and in the sacrificial system, God was both hidden and revealed, both near and present, both concealed and other. What do I mean here? The people were to approach the mountain (or the tent of meeting) and encounter the real and present God. But to encounter him would in no way diminish his majesty or reduce him to simply containable categories. He was not in this encounter revealed to be manipulable or domesticated (in contrast to the idols of the other nations). And so, to meet God at Sinai was to hear the thunder and see the lightning at the top of the mountain, and to hear his words through the mediation of Moses.

The entire system of Torah taught this lesson: that God was revealed to Israel but not contained by Israel. The Decalogue was and is itself a demonstration of this theological reality. The Ten Commandments are all about worship. In fact, worship is the key to understanding what they are really about. The first set of laws directed Israel's attention to the singularity and uniqueness of God and his demand for exclusive devotion—a devotion not in a manner that took his name "in vain" but as he directed. The hinge is the Sabbath command. It is the institution in the midst of the people's common life that recalls the divine work in the days of the creation—themselves a reminder of the saving acts of God.

The tabernacle and the Levitical code, with its system of priests and bloody sacrifices, became in time that remarkable symbol at the heart of the nation's life, the temple of Jerusalem. The notion of sacrifice and ritual was not unique to Israel, of course. Pagan cults of sacrifice abounded. Sacrifice was, in a sense, a familiar religious concept adapted for the expression of the particular theology of ancient Israel. To the pagan mind (illustrated amply by ancient literature—for example, in Homer's *Iliad*), sacrifice was the way by which the goodwill of the various gods was secured. Indeed, *security* was the underlying theme. Sacrifice was (to generalize) an act of taking out insurance against the contingencies of life in an uncertain world.

For Israel, sacrifice would be described as something else again. It was marked by a pattern of grace and gratitude: the pattern of rituals and festivals ensured that the narrative of the great acts of God for his people was not forgotten by them; and it enabled a response of thanksgiving for the blessings brought about by those acts. In addition, the sacrifices were a graphic illustration to Israel of the ebbing away of human life under the impact of sin. Being in the presence of God was not simply established by God moving closer; there was also the need for the atonement of sin. The shedding of blood for sin on the annual Day of Atonement was to purify the tabernacle and the people (Lev. 16). Peterson explains: "The life of an animal, represented by its blood splashed over the altar, is the ransom at the price of a life. Animal blood atones for human sin, not because of some magical quality or life-power in it but simply because God chose and prescribed it for this purpose."[7] Israel's response to God was on the basis of his prior revelation of himself and his redemption of them. But what was Israel given *to do*? They were to do homage to God; they were to serve him, and they were to revere him. These three biblical concepts are all yoked together under our English word *worship*.

First, *they were to do homage to God*. To "do homage" to another person is often indicated by a physical gesture, such as bowing or curtsying. The Old Testament vocabulary contains the sense of "bending over at the waist." But, of course, the outward gestures were expressions of an inner reality that could be expressed in all kinds of ways. The idea of the nations bowing down before YHWH (Ps. 22:27, 29) is a great vision of all the nations recognizing his kingly rule and authority. Thus the concept of worship as "doing homage" is not simply one of observing a physical gesture in a great display of submission to the rule of God but of actually enacting that rule as the reality in which one really believes. Nevertheless, this kind of worship *communicates*. It bears witness to a kind of relationship with God—to God and to others. It is an act, or a word, that speaks of God's rule.

Second, *they were to serve him*. A word frequently translated "worship" is the Greek *latreuō*, which has the connotation of "serve." The people of Israel were released from bondage to Pharaoh and called into the service of God (Ex. 3:12). The switch between these two kinds of bond-service is made clear in Deuteronomy 6:12–13: "Take care lest you forget the Lord, who brought you out

---

7. Peterson, *Engaging with God*, 41.

of the land of Egypt, out of the house of slavery. It is the LORD your God you shall fear. Him you shall serve and by his name you shall swear." This form of devotion to God involved the worshiper in an absolute sense.

> And now, Israel, what does the LORD your God require of you, but to fear the LORD your God, to walk in all his ways, to love him, to serve the LORD your God with all your heart and with all your soul, and to keep the commandments and statutes of the LORD, which I am commanding you today for your good? (Deut. 10:12–13)

Every aspect of the community's and the individual's life was to be marked by wholehearted and affectionate service of God by observing his commands. God is a great King who demands faithful obedience from his people. When this notion of service was extrapolated in relation to the rituals and ceremonies of ancient Israel, it did not lose the sense in which it was an observance of the true and just rule of God the King.

In the notions of homage and service, as the Bible treats them, we see a pattern developing—namely, that the worship of God includes the whole of the worshiper's life, but also specific acts and words of adoration. The one does not exclude the other, as if a life lived in a certain way were sufficient to embody true worship of Israel's God. This was partly because worship is, as we have already noted above, *communicative.* It does not merely do things at God's behest: it says things to him and about him. The literal act of offering homage becomes the metaphor by which a group of other activities is to be understood—and these activities can then be described as "worship."

Third, *the people were to revere or respect God.* The Hebrew notion of "the fear of the Lord" is included under this heading. It indicates not simply the performance of a particular set of gestures but also an attitude of heart. This disposition opens up the individual to the voice of the Lord (1 Sam. 12:14; Hag. 1:12) so as to do his will and to walk in his ways. In particular, the fear of the Lord is "the beginning of wisdom" (Prov. 9:10; see also 1:7). That is, the proper attitude to God, which respects his judgment on all people, inevitably leads to the wise human life.

A note of caution is advisable here, however. We are dealing with three overlapping concepts expressed in the vocabulary of the two biblical languages and placing them under the single heading of *worship*—an English word most often held to mean "pay homage to." The notion of service has accrued the sense of "worship" (and is frequently translated as such) precisely because of its usage in the context of the rituals and ceremonies of Israel. More precisely put, we might say that service has the character of worship, such that we can call it, by extension, "worship." In the right context, under the right conditions, a person's or a community's service can be an act of worship fully pleasing to God. But the primary sense of the English word remains the notion of adoration or homage.

Jesus Christ the One True Worshiper

In this brief sketch of the Old Testament account of worship, we have been able to see something of the pattern of the worship of YHWH that made it distinct from the idol worship of other nations. In particular, I have noted the pattern of *response to the divine initiative in specific acts and in the whole of life* that characterizes the worship of God's people. The problem with my account thus far has been that I have abstracted it from the history of Israel. The strong critiques of false worship with which we began should alert us to the fact that something is still incomplete in the account of worship given in the Hebrew Scriptures. Despite everything, Israel's life of worship became corrupted and diminished by the failure of the people to attend to the distinctive characteristics of the pattern of life they had been given. The final exile of Judah to Babylon was surrounded by a flurry of prophetic activity in which Israel's worship was both subjected to judgment and promised a renewal. The most terrible disaster of all was the utter destruction of the temple at this time, which meant the end to the God-ordained worship at that spot. What would worship look like without the temple and its ritual practices?

This was a crisis of worship. Ezekiel, for one, spoke of an extraordinary new temple with supernatural dimensions—one that would, somehow, replace the one destroyed by the Babylonians (Ezek. 40–48). The word "somehow" is deliberately chosen: for while the prophets foretold an intervention by God himself to restore the worshiping community of his people and to judge his enemies, they were not specific on the details. Isaiah spoke with poetic vigor about the "servant of the LORD" who would suffer for the iniquities of the people (Isa. 40–66); and many prophecies recalled the commitment of the covenant with David, that his line would be everlasting (2 Sam. 7; see, for example, Jeremiah's emphasis on Davidic kingship in Jer. 32–33).

Even given the divine initiative in engaging with people and the clarity of the pattern of response he demands—homage, service, reverence—the human response is inadequate. This is the point at which the New Testament claim is that in Jesus of Nazareth the history of Israel finds its fulfillment. Jesus is, of all human beings, the one who worships the God of Israel, the Creator of heaven and earth, as he demands to be worshiped—in purity and holiness. As the one human being who represents not simply Israel but all of humankind to the Father, he in himself enables a renovation of human worship. There is, following Christ, a significant continuity but a substantial discontinuity with Old Testament worship.

The notion of Jesus as the true worshiper is reflected across the New Testament but finds itself refracted in particular through the imagery of the new temple and the declaration of a new covenant. In light of these, the New Testament authors felt able still to speak of the Christian life, individually and corporately, in terms that echoed the worship language of the Old Testament. Jesus's encounter with the devil in the wilderness, recorded in detail by Matthew and Luke, features an interchange over the subject of worship:

The devil took him to a very high mountain and showed him all
the kingdoms of the world and their glory. And he said to him,
"All these I will give you, if you will fall down and worship me."
Then Jesus said to him, "Be gone, Satan! For it is written,

"'You shall worship the Lord your God
and him only shall you serve.'" (Matt. 4:8–10)

The devil offers global power and authority in exchange for
Jesus's homage ("fall down and worship"). Surely there's an ironic
element to the exchange: would Jesus really possess the right to
rule if he had to bow down to another? Jesus's response, like his
responses to the other temptations, is to lean hard on the word of
God—in this case, the exclusive worship demanded by the Lord in
Deuteronomy 6:13. Jesus's act of submission to God, or rather his
refusal of submission to the evil one, is shown to us to establish his
credentials as the true worshiper.

The disruption that Jesus's ministry causes, which apparently
leads to his death, is chiefly the result of his operating from within
the temple as a strong critic of the contemporary temple life. In
Matthew, Mark, and John he is heard prophesying the destruction of the temple and claiming that he can rebuild it in three days.
John, in particular, picks up the language of God's presence and his
glory, which is reminiscent of what the Israelites expected from the
tabernacle and the temple: "And the Word became flesh and dwelt
among us, and we have seen his glory, glory as of the only Son from
the Father, full of grace and truth" (John 1:14).

Jesus takes the prophetic vision of the new temple and, extraordinarily, shows how he himself realizes that hope in his life, death,
resurrection, and ascension. The temple as the location for the
encounter between God and his people is, in Jesus, relocated. In
him, the need for sacrifice to prepare the people for meeting God is
obviated. The source for the renewal and restoration of Israel and,
by extension, "all the families of the earth" is now Jesus himself—
which is the prompt for the inclusion of the Gentiles. Engaging

with God is now mediated to human beings in the person and work of Jesus Christ, which in turn shows that the temple was merely a foretaste of what has now appeared in human history.

At the same time, as Jesus is the means through which people are to come to worship God "in spirit and truth" (John 4:24), Jesus has also become himself the worthy object of homage. I hinted previously that this is, in many ways, the most difficult theological problem that the New Testament authors have to face. How can a strict monotheism such as Judaic faith give birth to, or be held to pave the way for, a faith in which veneration is offered to (apparently) more than one divine person? And yet, the heart of the New Testament gospel is the declaration "Jesus is Lord," a statement of homage that ascribes an authority to him that only a divine person deserves (Rom. 10:9; 1 Cor. 12:3). The New Testament answer is to speak about Jesus's unity with the Father (1 Cor. 8:6; Eph. 4:4–7).

Jesus also portrays himself, and is portrayed as, the inheritor and fulfillment of the pattern of covenantal relationship with God that stretches back to Abraham. As with the temple, the ministry of Jesus is felt to be a critique of the law by his opponents, and they take great offense. Yet a more careful reading of his words and actions shows him to be a skilled interpreter and advocate of the law. He is not rejecting it; he is rather meeting its requirements and transcending it. He is, he claims, inaugurating a new covenant (something promised in Jeremiah's prophecy—Jer. 31:31–34). At the Last Supper, he makes explicit the link between his sacrificial death and the notion of a new covenant (language picked up in Heb. 9:14–15)—pointing thereby to what worship will now mean: namely, that he will make true worship of God possible by means of his atoning blood, and that he will thereby be the focus of the homage of the new covenant people.

The theology of the book of Hebrews adds another aspect to the New Testament's Christological account of worship. In particular, it places Christ as the present heavenly mediator of our worship. He lives forever to intercede for us (Heb. 6:20; 7:25–28;

8:6).[8] Hebrews takes the great Old Testament theology of atonement, as it was expressed in the Day of Atonement ceremonies, and uses it to explain the work of Jesus Christ for us in enabling our engagement with God. The high priest represented the people to God, consecrated and purified for the ministry of sacrifice by rituals of washing and bloody sprinkling. Then he offered the sacrificial victim as a substitute for the people as an object of the divine wrath against sin. In Hebrews, it is Jesus who is one with the people, "not ashamed to call them brothers" (Heb. 2:12); and it is he who is cleansed and made perfect in the course of his life: "one who in every respect has been tempted as we are, yet without sin" (Heb. 4:15). He offers a sacrifice for sin—this time not an animal, but himself, in order to bear in his own person the penalty for sin. But being vindicated by the God who raised him from the dead, he now is our forerunner into the presence of God—not only as the one who brings God closer to human beings by being the presence of God among us but also as the Spirit-filled and sanctified human who is able to bring human beings close to God. James Torrance explains:

It is supremely in Jesus Christ that we see the double meaning of grace. Grace means that God gives himself to us as God, freely and unconditionally, to be worshiped and adored. But grace also means that God comes to us in Jesus Christ as man, to do for us and in us what we cannot do. He offers a life of perfect obedience and worship and prayer to the Father, that we might be drawn by the Spirit into communion with the Father, "through Jesus Christ our Lord."[9]

The great evangel, then, demands that those who hear the good news acknowledge Jesus as Lord—that they worship him. The gospel is a call to worship. And yet, it is also a declaration that, in Jesus,

8. James Torrance, *Worship, Community, and the Triune God of Grace*, Didsbury Lectures (Carlisle: Paternoster, 1996), 35.
9. Torrance, *Worship*, 55.

we have one who represents us as worshipers—one who worships on our behalf in the throne room of God.

The Worship of the Triune God

We find, then, in the New Testament a reminder that worship is a response to the gracious divine initiative and that it is enabled by God. But we find that the mediatory means of the Old Testament—the temple, the sacrificial system, the Torah—are now made redundant by the new and singular focus and locus for worship, Jesus Christ himself. The theological reflection already beginning in the pages of the New Testament about the unity of Jesus Christ with the Father flowers into the new and distinctively Christian identification of God as triune. This is naturally of considerable importance for an understanding of the notion of Christian worship since it relates to *who* is being worshiped. The Christian answer becomes *the one God who is Father, Son, and Holy Spirit.*

Worshiping the God who is triune makes a substantial difference to what true worship actually is.[10] The doctrine of the Trinity means that Christian worship is a sharing in the Son's union with his Father, through the Holy Spirit. Our union with Christ in the power of the Holy Spirit is the basis for this sharing of God's people together in the divine life of God. We stand to worship God by means of the mediatory ministry of Jesus before the Father, to which we are drawn by the fellowship of the Holy Spirit. As our great high priest, he sanctifies us by his blood, which he himself offered. This understanding of our relationship to the triune God was in part responsible for the Reformation's rejection of the medieval concept of priesthood—since Christ is our supreme and exclusive mediator before God. As Torrance puts it, "The doctrine of the Trinity is the grammar of this participatory understanding of worship and prayer."[11]

---

10. For what follows, see Torrance, *Worship*, chap. 1.
11. Torrance, *Worship*, 9.

There are two faulty (but sadly common) alternatives to the Trinitarian understanding of worship. The first is that of Protestant liberalism as represented by such thinkers as the great nineteenth-century German historian of the church Adolf von Harnack and the twentieth-century British theologian John Hick. Essentially, on this view, religion is about each soul's individual and immediate relationship to God. Jesus, like Israel, had a direct encounter with the divine that is the model for our encounter with God today. Jesus does not mediate worship; he simply exemplifies it. He is certainly not the object of worship.

Naturally, this view of worship is a direct attack on the doctrine of the Trinity, since it has no place (and no need) for a representative or substitutionary act of atonement to reconcile human beings to God. It has no need to proclaim the church as a fellowship of the Spirit, since the emphasis is entirely on the individual's dealings directly with the divine. It results in a moralistic Christianity—noble in its aspiration for the human spirit but doomed to fall on the barbed wire of no-man's-land in World War I.

The second faulty alternative focuses instead on existential experience in the present day. The German New Testament scholar Rudolf Bultmann is an exponent of this view, although it has had its impact on Christianity at a popular level. The work of Christ for us is not denied; indeed, it is essential on this view. But it is connected to us through the event of faith arising in us, which becomes the emphasis. What Jesus did is more important than, or disconnected from, who he was. The doctrines of the incarnation and of the Trinity fade in importance, and my own religious experience surfaces. Much contemporary Christianity is fixated by the search for individual religious experience. The language of "a personal relationship with God" can be distorted in this direction, with talk about *my* conversion, *my* decision, and *my* response. The reduction of Christian worship to this two-dimensional system—meaning that it is just about me and God here now—communicates simply that our response is what really matters. What it overlooks, says Torrance, is that, in Christ, God has "provided for us that Response which alone is acceptable to him—the offering made for the whole human race in the life, obedience and passion of Jesus Christ."[12]

The witness of the gospels is to a very different form of worship. Jesus is, above all, depicted as having a unique relationship with the Father—signaled at his baptism by his anointing by the Holy Spirit and the declaration of the divine favor ("this is my beloved Son"— Matt. 3:17; see also Mark 1:11; Luke 3:22). This is the Spirit who is poured out on the people of God at Pentecost, so enabling them to share in the fellowship, or communion, between the Father and the Son. In the words of John, "Indeed our fellowship is with the Father and with his Son Jesus Christ" (1 John 1:3).

Communion with God the Father in Christ by the Holy Spirit is thus the fundamental—and only—basis for a doctrine of the church, and by extension, the only basis for an understanding of its corporate practices of worship. Like Israel, the church is constituted and given an identity on the basis of nothing other than the work of God. The church is the church of the Holy Trinity: called by the Father, purified by the Son, and gathered together by the Holy Spirit. As Peter writes, "Once you were not a people, but now you are God's people; once you had not received mercy, but now you have received mercy" (1 Pet. 2:10). Note the parallelism: the basis for the common identity of the church is the mercy that comes through the grace of God in Christ Jesus and his mercy-bringing death. Peter's opening address to the scattered believers illustrates their Trinitarian constitution: ". . . according to the foreknowledge of God the Father, in the sanctification of the Spirit, for obedience to Jesus Christ and for sprinkling with his blood" (1 Pet. 1:2).

If this is the theological architecture of the church, then what difference does it make for how we understand our acts of worship—or indeed, for how we decide what acts of worship in fact are? The people of God are still called, as of old, to "proclaim the excel-

12. Torrance, *Worship*, 18.

lencies of him who called [them] out of darkness into his marvelous light" (1 Pet. 2:9). They meet on the basis of the lordship of Christ articulated through his merciful sacrifice and in the knowledge that he stands as a perfect mediator between them and God. They are enabled, then, to draw near to God confident in the prior working of God in drawing near to them in Christ. They can view their adoration of God as a sacrifice fully pleasing to him (Heb. 13:15–16).

The distinction that we sometimes observe in English between "corporate" and "individual" worship is actually a false one, since worship of the triune God by definition brings the individual believer into communion with others. There is no non-church, non-corporate worship. And, while it is important to note the emphasis in the New Testament on all of life as worship (as in the Old), that worshipful life, indicative of membership in Christ, is therefore indicative of membership of Christ's body. Romans 12:1 is a key text here, often used to argue that the New Testament emphasis is on individual acts as worship and not what is done in the church gathering: "I appeal to you therefore, brothers, by the mercies of God, to present your bodies as a living sacrifice, holy and acceptable to God, which is your spiritual worship."

We should notice right away the use of sacrificial language to describe the activity of believers. Of course, we read this in the light of Paul's emphatic description of Jesus's atoning sacrifice in Romans 3:21–31; there can be no sense in which our sacrifice plays the role of establishing our relationship with God. But in Romans 12:1, Paul envisages a sacrifice of the believers' bodies that is now in fact pleasing to God—something made possible by Christ's prior atoning sacrifice.[13] And this "is your spiritual worship." Almost all English translations deploy the word *worship* to translate *latreia* (not *proskyneō*). That is, the word for service rather than homage is here used. Since only one of the concepts usually contained under the linguistic domain of *worship* is here being used, it seems

---

13. A similar thought pattern is found in Heb. 13:15–16.

a stretch to build an entire theology of Christian worship on the basis of this verse. Nevertheless, the verse uses cultic language to talk not about ritual activity but about behavior in a way that echoes Hosea 6:6:

> For I desire steadfast love and not sacrifice,
>   the knowledge of God rather than burnt offerings.

The language of cultic service/worship is now used to describe Christ's work and, secondarily, the mutual and sacrificial service of Christians for one another. There is no Christian form of the cult.

But we should also note how richly ecclesial Paul's exposition of his command is here, following as it does from his extraordinary account of the people of God in Romans 9–11. The pronouns in 12:1 are plural: the "spiritual worship" is "your" act in the sense that it is collectively the worshipful act of the entire community. The rest of chapter 12 moves on to an exploration of the unity-in-distinction of the body of Christ: "For as in one body we have many members, and the members do not all have the same function, so we, though many, are one body in Christ, and individually members one of another" (Rom. 12:4–5).

The body motif is foundational to Paul's Trinitarian ecclesiology, and he repeats it in 1 Corinthians 12. The unity of the church is not simply a mirror of the divine unity but comes about through the enfolding of the members of the church into Christ by the Spirit of God. The worship of this people—which is an echo of, but not a replacement for, Christ's worship of the Father—includes their costly and forgiving love for one another. It is entirely appropriate, therefore, to call the gathering of the people of God "worship," since the earthly gathering of a congregation gives expression to the identity they have already received in Christ, and since in their meeting together they anticipate the final, heavenly gathering, in which the triune God is adored forevermore. In Christ, God's people meet together to meet with him: to adore him, to revere him, and to serve him as they give themselves in mutual service of one another in anticipation of the final in-gathering of God's people. This eschatological theme is borne out in the depictions of heavenly worship in the book of Revelation (Rev. 4, 5) and in Hebrews 12:

> But you have come to Mount Zion and to the city of the living God, the heavenly Jerusalem, and to innumerable angels in festal gathering, and to the assembly of the firstborn who are enrolled in heaven, and to God, the judge of all, and to the spirits of the righteous made perfect, and to Jesus, the mediator of a new covenant, and to the sprinkled blood that speaks a better word than the blood of Abel. (Heb. 12:22–24)

The work of the Holy Spirit in the church is to point to this final consummation, as a "guarantee" (2 Cor. 1:21–22).

The Consequences of Christian Worship

God's people are able to pay homage to him as a result of their union in Christ, who cleanses them by his blood and leads them in adoration of God. They are enabled to worship God because God has gathered them together and given them his name. They submit to him as Lord in listening to his word and seeking to encounter him there. Their adoration of the triune Lord is to be reflected in wholehearted and sacrificial service of one another—spiritual acts of worship now, in Christ, pleasing to him. In succeeding chapters, we will examine in turn how the various components of Christian worship—preaching, sacraments, prayer, and music—reflect the theological reality of the church as a worshiping community. For now, I shall take the opportunity to explore three substantial implications of Christian worship.

The first of these is *the edification of God's people*. In 1 Corinthians 14, which is one of the few passages of the New Testament where church meetings are actually discussed, Paul connects the gifts of the Spirit with the "building up" of the body. The gifts are given for that particular purpose, such that the gathering of God's people ought to be ordered accordingly: "What then, brothers?

When you come together, each one has a hymn, a lesson, a revelation, a tongue, or an interpretation. Let all things be done for building up" (1 Cor. 14:26). Ephesians 4 is the other passage with a similar concern. "Building up" has the sense of the maturing and strengthening of the whole, particularly (in Eph. 4) in unity. The leadership offices of apostle, teacher, and so on are (once more) provided for this purpose. As the believers meet together in the fellowship of the Spirit to engage with the Father by the blood of the Son, they are built up, collectively, in love for one another (Eph. 4:16).

The second consequence is that Christian corporate worship is *political*. One author puts it this way:

> In the celebration of worship the congregation is transposed into a particular social order. . . . Christ is the head of the Church, and the life of the communities of his people follows the law of his Spirit. In this respect it is inescapably political—aligned towards the recognition of the good that comes from God, towards the common exploration of the good in the world and towards the common exploration of that good in shared action.[14]

Here is a strong case that in the celebration of worship Christians become a social order of a particular kind: the body of the risen Lord. Life in this community is definitely ruled—that is, by (the word of) its Lord. It then has a pattern of life that it learns in response to this rule. The Spirit of God gathers the congregation, which then pays homage to Jesus *specifically as Lord* in its common activities. It is at this point that the political dimension arises: this particular sharing forms a specific kind of community in which "believers find their basic political existence."[15]

The gathering of the Christian community in worship has a specifically political character; it is the formation of a political form of life. This runs counter, of course, to the contemporary secular

---

14. Bernd Wannenwetsch and Margaret Kohl, *Political Worship: Ethics for Christian Citizens* (Oxford: Oxford University Press, 2004), 9.

15. Wannenwetsch and Kohl, *Political Worship*, 7.

view that seeks to privatize faith as "spirituality," and specifically to depoliticize it. The experience of membership in the church, with all it entails, must inevitably (as it has historically) inform the Christian's citizenship—over against the totalizing claims of liberal society, if necessary.

Gathering together in the name of the Son of God, Christians foreshadow the final rule of God in Christ. This immediately relativizes the absolute claims of worldly powers, which frequently see this as a threat. The court tales from the book of Daniel are a case in point, stories that were often cited by the martyrs of the early Christian era. For example, the great image of gold set up by Nebuchadnezzar in Daniel 2 is raised as an object of religious worship, but the political ramifications are clear. This is the tyrant's statue, and refusal to worship his statue is not simply blasphemy but treason. When the three young Jewish men Shadrach, Meshach, and Abednego refuse to worship the statue because of their exclusive commitment to worship the God of Israel, the rage of Nebuchadnezzar reveals how threatened he is. Their refusal is a direct challenge to his supreme authority.

In all kinds of ways, the practices generated by Christian worship form a new, redeemed way of being a people. Since Christ is Lord, human authority is seen as derived from him and ultimately subject to him, and we learn to respect but not to fear it. Since Christ is Lord, we learn to live a life rich in thanksgiving and generosity in a world full of the worship of mammon. Since Christ is Lord and since we participate together in him, we learn by painful practice what suffering for another's sake means. Since Christ is Lord, we learn that ethnic and class distinctions do not form the measure of humankind. These are all directly political lessons that spring from Christian worship.

The third ramification of Christian worship is *mission*. Christian worship is *missional*. As I have already indicated, worship is a *communicative* or *expressive* act. It expresses the allegiance and submission of the worshiper to the worshiped one. Christian worship, enabled by God himself and empowered by the Spirit, is not simply for the sake of God's pleasure. It exists as a testimony to call those who do not yet worship. First Peter 2:9–10 is instructive: "But you are a chosen race, a royal priesthood, a holy nation, a people for his own possession, that you may proclaim the excellencies of him who called you out of darkness into his marvelous light" (1 Pet. 2:9). In this verse, which applies categories by which Israel was described at Sinai (e.g., "a kingdom of priests"—Ex. 19:6), Peter casts the new covenant people of God in the role of those who proclaim the mighty acts of God to the world. Just as they had once existed in darkness and nonidentity, so now they speak of the glory of God to those who are without hope in the world. They are "priests" in the sense that their form of life mediates God's character to the outside world, and they become in their form of life the location at which those far off may now be drawn near. By observing their form of life, the nations are to be led to pay homage to God: "Keep your conduct among the Gentiles honorable, so that when they speak against you as evildoers, they may see your good deeds and glorify God on the day of visitation" (1 Pet. 2:12). In 1 Corinthians 14, Paul urges the Corinthians to value the intelligibility of prophecy in their corporate worship over the cacophony and confusion of tongues-speaking: "But if all prophesy, and an unbeliever or outsider enters, he is convicted by all, he is called to account by all, the secrets of his heart are disclosed, and so, falling on his face, he will worship God and declare that God is really among you" (1 Cor. 14:24–25).

The outsider's worship springs as a consequence from the gathered activity of the congregation. The worship of God's people, directed to the God who saved them and made them what they are, takes place in and before the watching world. It has a secondary audience. The great acts of God are rehearsed not simply for his sake but also for the sake of those who have never heard them told.

CHAPTER 2

Worship in the English Reformation

For we think it convenient that every country should use such ceremonies, as they shall think best to the setting forth of God's honour and glory, and to the reducing of the people to a most perfect and godly living, without error or superstition; and that they should put away other things, which from time to time they perceive to be most abused, as in men's ordinances it often chanceth diversely in diverse countries.

"On Ceremonies, why some be abolished and some remain," 1549 Book of Common Prayer[1]

Is there anything distinctive about a Reformation Anglican view of Christian worship? Having presented an account of Christian worship drawn from Scripture in chapter 1, I now want to give an outline of the major theological themes of the English Reformation and to link them to the changes in liturgy and piety that were brought about in that period.

---

1. Quoted in Joseph Ketley, ed., *Two Liturgies . . . of Edward VI* (Cambridge: Parker Society, 1844), 157.

Looking to Scripture for guidance, Thomas Cranmer had a very deliberate idea of what authentic Christian worship was, and he saw the Book of Common Prayer as the practical expression of that idea in the unique conditions of mid-sixteenth-century England. He also had a very particular idea of what forms of worship most certainly did *not* fit that description. Edification was the key measure of authentic Christian worship for Cranmer as it was for the other leaders of the European Reformation.

It was Martin Luther who pioneered the idea that Christian worship was not about what the people did for God but about what God did for the people. The characteristic pre-Reformation notion of worship had been precisely the opposite—namely, that the people gathered in order for the priest to offer a sacrifice to God on their behalf. But when the people came together under the influence of the Reformers, it was to hear the proclamation of the gospel through which God would work in people's hearts and minds. Reformation worship was where people presented their hearts to Christ and he performed spiritual surgery on them, cleansing them and filling them with loving gratitude so that they desired to and were enabled to give him praise with their lips and lives. And, as we shall see, Cranmer conceived of edification in terms of order and understanding—so that Holy Scripture might be allowed to do its work on the congregation, by the power of God's Spirit. Edification was God's work in the people through Scripture.

Dissolving the Chantries

It would be easy to forget the context in which Thomas Cranmer began to prepare his new liturgies for the English people. The Edwardian program for Protestantizing the English church was very much in full swing; and it included a very significant piece of legislation: the 1547 Act Dissolving the Chantries. The chantry houses and parish chapels had been, until this moment, a prominent feature of English religious life, representing an extensive industry in prayer. In the church's second millennium, notable and wealthy persons had founded monasteries whose chief task was the saying of Masses for the souls of the dead, based on the belief that doing so would mitigate the punishment of the deceased in purgatory and speed them toward the beatific vision. The Cluniac order, in particular, had developed a liturgy for the dead and received huge financial endowments for this purpose.

At first, the endowing of chantries was the province of kings alone, since they alone could afford to fund a Mass to be said for their souls in perpetuity. By the later Middle Ages, however, it was common practice for people of all kinds to leave some level of funds for the saying of a Mass for their souls—even if it was just for a year. Eamon Duffy notes, "Bequests for short-term chantries of this sort, usually for periods from one to seven years, formed an important element in the religious economy of many communities."[2]

That not much had changed by 1547 was indicated by Henry VIII's own will. In his last will and testament, made on December 30, 1546, he stipulated that "an altar shall be furnished for the saying of daily masses while the world shall endure."[3]

All monasteries had been dissolved by Henry VIII by 1540, a move which was arguably as much about seizing their substantial assets for the royal coffers as it was about theological conviction. Henry had also observed that the monasteries were centers of opposition to royal supremacy in the church. The wording of the 1547 act, if taken at face value, reveals that a similar mix of financial expediency and a different theological outlook was at work in the demise of the chantries:

> The king's most loving subjects, the Lords spiritual and temporal, and the Commons, in this present Parliament assembled, considering that a great part of superstition and errors in the Christian religion has been brought into the minds and

---

2. Eamon Duffy, *The Stripping of the Altars: Traditional Religion in England, c. 1400–c. 1580* (New Haven, CT: Yale University Press, 1992), 369.

3. Peter Marshall, *Beliefs and the Dead in Reformation England* (Oxford: Oxford University Press, 2002), 91.

estimations of men, by reason of the ignorance of their very true and perfect salvation through the death of Jesus Christ, and by devising and phantasing vain opinions of purgatory and masses satisfactory, to be done for them which be departed, the which doctrine and vain opinion by nothing more is maintained and upholden, than by the abuse of trentals, chantries, and other provisions made for the continuance of the said blindness and ignorance . . . [4]

The act plainly states that the enormous funds by now tied up in the chantries were to be diverted to the public good—to schools, universities, and the poor. It is doubtful that this ever occurred. King Edward grammar schools were eventually set up, but much of the money went into the war against Scotland. However, the theological rationale for the dissolution was also plainly stated in the act: namely, that the "very true and perfect salvation through the death of Jesus Christ" was now no longer to be obscured by the religion of purgatory and the saying of Masses. The entire economic structure propped up by the theology of purgatory and the notion that the saying of Masses could make satisfaction for the sins of the dead was now to be undone, because an alternative proposition was now in view that made redundant the old way. The death of Christ obviated all other supposed means of satisfaction for sin. The prayers of the living could not alter the status of the souls of the departed, since such prayers could not of themselves be held to be meritorious in any way.

It is worth starting our consideration of the worship of Reformation Anglicanism by noting what it was clearly *against*. In "On Ceremonies," Cranmer very clearly stands against medieval theology and liturgy insofar as it obscured and indeed contradicted the gospel. "On Ceremonies" was a strong *no* to the dominant piety of medieval Catholic England with its veneration of saints, its saying

---

4. Henry Gee and William John Hardy, *Documents Illustrative of English Church History* (London: Macmillan, 1896), 328–29. A "trental" was a set of thirty Masses said to aid the passage of a recently deceased loved one through purgatory.

of Masses for the dead, its sacred objects, and its ornate worship. The polemic against the practices of worship that adhered to the old theology is as notable as the construction of a new form of worship to replace it. Of course, it is customary today to note the continuity between the English church of the medieval period and its sixteenth-century counterpart, rehearsing, among other points, the use Cranmer made of the Sarum Missal,[5] in order to resist the Reformation propaganda that would overstate the difference. However, it remains indisputable that Cranmer's liturgies represent a very major break with what went before in the theory and practice of corporate worship. The Edwardian policy of gradual alterations allowed for the appearance of continuity as a strategy for change management. Cranmer was comfortable with the old forms of worship if they could be adapted to serve the proclamation of the gospel.

What exactly was being rejected in the dissolution of the chantries? It was a wholesale rejection of the theological system that underpinned them. The doctrine of purgatory and its associated practices were, to the Reformers, only symptoms of a deeper malaise. In the introduction to Cranmer's *Defence of the True and Catholic Doctrine of the Sacrament of the Body and Blood of Christ*, he was clear that rooting out the notion of the Mass as a sacrifice was the most important fundamental reform the Church of England had to make, because all other errors sprang from it.[6] That malady, as he saw it, had been diagnosed brilliantly by Martin Luther and the other Continental Reformers from 1517 onward, and it was this: that the soteriology of the medieval church rested on faulty, unscriptural premises and involved at once an overoptimistic assessment of the human condition, a misunderstanding of the role and nature of the death of Jesus in our salvation, and ultimately a problematic doctrine of God. It was no surprise that the worship which resulted from such grave errors was full of superstition and

---

5. The Sarum Missal was the Latin liturgy for the Mass most widely used in medieval England.

6. Henry Jenkyns, ed., *The Remains of Thomas Cranmer*, 4 vols. (Oxford: Oxford University Press, 1833), 2:289.

corruption. Luther's famous tirades against Johannes Tetzel, the well-known seller of indulgences, frothed over from his new conviction not simply that Tetzel was a greedy charlatan who used extensive emotional manipulation to defraud poor peasants but also that the theological error he was promulgating endangered people's very souls.

Martin Luther's Breakthrough

Luther and those who followed him fought a war on two fronts. First, he was making a material claim about how people received salvation that was a complete challenge to the prevailing understandings in medieval Europe. Luther's own spiritual journey was a quest to find a righteousness in God that would not simply crush him as a sinful human being. He learned from Augustine how intractable human sinfulness was. But none of the medieval explanations for how salvation subsequently occurred seemed to factor in the depths of human sin. All of them, in one way or another, seemed to rely on human beings taking a step in some way toward the divine to make themselves worthy of God's love. And yet, as Luther read Scripture and examined his own soul in the quiet of his monastic cell, he could not see how any such step was possible.

This led Luther to his great breakthrough as he lectured on the Bible in the classroom and prayed to God in his despair. He realized that, according to Scripture, God justifies sinners neither on account of any meritorious action they have performed, whether good work or religious rite, nor even on the basis of a willingness to do good, but purely on account of the blood of Jesus Christ shed on behalf of the ungodly. The believer has simply the task of repenting and believing the good news. This faith, which binds the believer to Christ "our righteousness," is to be understood not as a virtue, or merely as a giving of assent, but as an offering of oneself in trust. It is nothing, but in a sense also everything: it is giving oneself entirely to the promises of God in utter dependence on him and in the realization that there is nothing of our own we can offer him.

The fundamental basis of this theology of free justification of sinners was the predestined grace of God. Luther had come to this understanding, as I said, on the basis of his reading and rereading of Scripture—and this is the second of the two fronts on which Luther fought, the Reformation's formal principle. Aided by the revival of classical learning fostered by scholars like Erasmus of Rotterdam, Scripture reading could now be done in the original languages instead of in the Latin translation of Jerome. This new access to the text brought a number of flaws in Jerome's translation to the notice of scholarly Europe. The most significant of these was Jerome's translation of the Greek word *metanoiete* as "do penance," rather than "repent." "To do penance" was understood in terms of the penitential system of the institutional church, and spawned an entire framework of piety involving acts of self-punishment and self-abasement as a preparation for the work of grace. "Repentance," on the other hand, simply indicates a turning of the person to receive the grace of God. In Jesus's preaching it formed a pair with believing the good news (Matt. 3:2). Here he declared that repenting and believing were the same action, or, at least, two sides of the same action. This was a decisive blow to the medieval system of salvation and the practices of worship that surrounded it, since that worship was part of seeking to please God with some meritorious act.

But it was not simply that a different theology was being uncovered from the pages of Scripture by a better process of translation. An entirely different view of Scripture and its role in salvation of individuals and in the doctrine of the church began to emerge in the 1520s. This was a distinctly different view of how the grace of God would be mediated to human beings. If one is justified by *faith*, and this faith comes from hearing the gracious gospel as it is contained in Scripture, then the focus for our piety ought clearly to be Scripture itself, since that is the avenue of God's arrival. In that book and by those words is Christ communicated to men and women, and not by some other means. Certainly, it is not through sacred objects, nor through acts of mystical worship focused on something other than

the message of Scripture: these are, if anything, spiritually dangerous distractions from the main business. The divine-human encounter takes place as the gospel is presented and the message of the
grace of God in Christ is revived, and not on some other stage. God is
met through ruminating on his written word. The words of Scripture
could and should be read or heard by anyone, without the mediation
of the church—which, after all, had proved itself quite fallible.

The impact of this theological revolution on forms of corporate
worship in the Continental centers of the Reformation varied enor-
mously in style, but they shared some crucial elements. Luther himself wrote: "We are to sacrifice nothing else to God than trust and
hope in him. . . . The forgiveness of sins and grace are greater than
the whole world's act of worship. . . . The best and most appropriate worship of God is to trust and believe. And he demands nothing
more than a heart that believes in him."[7]

The result of this new outlook was a fresh emphasis on the vernacular language in liturgy and on the reading of Scripture; a more
prominent place for the preaching of the word (reflected in changes
in church architecture and furnishing); the use of congregational
hymnody as an act of worship and an educational tool (Zwingli and
Luther themselves penned hymns); and, despite profound disagreements as to the nature of the Lord's Supper, an entirely different
role for it in the life of the Christian—now to nourish faith rather
than to mechanically gain meritorious grace.

The English Break from Rome

Henry VIII was not quick to embrace Luther's teachings on faith
and worship. In fact, the king publicly repudiated both in his anti-
Lutheran book *An Assertion of the Seven Sacraments* (1521). For
Henry's defense of traditionalist religion, the pope awarded him
the title "Defender of the Faith." Yet, toward the end of the same
decade the king grew increasingly more restless under the papacy

---

7. Cited in D. A. Carson and World Evangelical Fellowship, *Worship: Adoration and Action* (Grand Rapids, MI: Baker, 1993), 133.

because of Clement VII's refusal to annul his marriage to Katherine of Aragon. As Henry's "great matter" emerged as the political crisis of the late 1520s and early 1530s, university intellectuals who had been influenced by arguments for the primacy of Scripture were a ready source of aid to Henry in his wrangle with the pope, including the Cambridge lecturer Thomas Cranmer. Henry's appointment of Cranmer to the see of Canterbury at the end of 1532, whether the king realized it or not, gave respectability, credibility, and a political boost to the authority of Scripture over the teachings of the church, and not only on the issue of the divorce but also on justification. For it was probably earlier that year that Cranmer himself had become a convinced evangelical, during his time as Henry's ambassador to Germany, where he encountered Lutheran theology firsthand.

However, the break with Rome in 1534 signaled not, by any means, the triumph of evangelical ideas in England but the beginning of their wider dissemination. Deeply influenced by his time in Germany, Cranmer began to push for change in the Bible's role in worship. The Scriptures were now to be translated into the vernacular as an official policy endorsed by the king himself. This came too late for the hapless William Tyndale, who was burned at the stake in what we now call Belgium in 1536. Nevertheless, his translation of Scripture, a work carried out furtively and at great personal cost, became the basis for the official version of the Great Bible. Tyndale's vision of the common Englishman or Englishwoman reading the Scriptures in his or her own language—and worshiping God without the mediation of the church—would begin to see fulfillment shortly after he was executed. If hearing the gospel of Jesus Christ in the Bible and responding in faith were the essence of Christian piety, then the English church should take care to make sure that this gospel was declared by its ministers and heard by its congregations. In his preface to the Great Bible (1540) Cranmer heralded a return to a new kind of piety, which was reflective of the practice of the early church, emphasizing the teaching of Scripture to all people:

In the scriptures be the fat pastures of the soul. . . . He that is ignorant, shall find there what he should learn. He that is a perverse sinner, shall there find his damnation to make him to tremble for fear. He that laboureth to serve God, shall find there his glory, and the [promises] of eternal life, exhorting him more diligently to labour. Herein may princes learn how to govern their subjects; subjects obedience, love and dread to their princes: husbands how they should behave them unto their wives; how to educate their children and servants; and contrary the wives, children, and servants may know their duty to their husbands, parents and masters.[8]

The old piety was not yet ready to be eradicated, however. As the Cambridge historian Eamon Duffy has shown by extensive research, the English people were in great part sincerely devoted and deeply committed to the faith in which they had grown up.[9] There were underground pockets of evangelical faith; but as far as the English people were concerned, the Reformation was yet to take hold in all but a political sense. The dissolution of the monasteries, engineered by Thomas Cromwell from 1536 onward, was not quite what the populace had been waiting for all along. Nonetheless, the attack on the monastic way of life would alter the spirituality of England forever. Henry had complex motives for eradicating them. The financial rewards were attractive. However, influenced by Erasmian humanism, he was not much pleased with the monasteries as centers of the superstitious devotion to relics. But he was also keen to stamp out cells of opposition to his supremacy. The end of monasteries also signaled a determination on the part of the evangelicals to work toward establishing the worship of the English people on a completely different footing from thence forward, where saving faith, rather than good works, was at the center of Christian piety.

---

8. Cited in Gordon Jeanes, "Cranmer and Common Prayer," in *The Oxford Guide to the Book of Common Prayer: A Worldwide Survey*, ed. Charles C. Hefling and Cynthia L. Shattuck (Oxford: Oxford University Press, 2006), 22–23.

9. See Eamon Duffy, *The Stripping of the Altars: Traditional Religion in England 1400–1580*, 2nd ed. (New Haven, CT: Yale University Press, 2005).

The Edwardian Liturgies

The death of King Henry in 1547 was the opportunity to pursue the renovation of English worship in earnest, and Cranmer busied himself with the task. He would seek to transform the way in which English Christians thought of themselves as encountering God. Writes Ashley Null, "In his prayers for the English people Cranmer gradually enshrined turning to God in repentance and faith as the chief effect of saving grace and its chief means."[10]

The 1549 prayer book contained two statements, "A Preface" and "Of Ceremonies Omitted or Retained," in which Cranmer explained the rationale for his new liturgy.[11] In "A Preface," he outlined his understanding of the decline of common worship in the church. In the first instance, Cranmer noted that the patristic practice of reading systematically through the Bible had been lost and needed to be recovered. This was an example of the classic evangelical claim that they were in continuity with patristic theology and practice. The "godly and decent order of the ancient fathers" had, for Cranmer, become corrupted by the addition of all kinds of extra pieces of liturgy and complicated rules such that "many times there was more business to find out what should be read, than to read it when it was found out." Who could complain about a simplification of the rules for common prayer? Who would find unreasonable the suggestion that "now from henceforth, all the whole realm shall have but one use"? The explanation given seems to mask somewhat the shift in theological position at the heart of the new form of service by pointing to the practical advantages of a tidied-up book.

In the second piece, "Of Ceremonies," subtitled "Why Some Be Abolished, and Some Retained," Cranmer outlined a defense of his policy of liturgical reform. He was not opposed to the invention or addition of man-made ceremonies per se. Some such ceremonies,

---

10. Ashley Null, *Thomas Cranmer's Doctrine of Repentance: Renewing the Power to Love* (Oxford: Oxford University Press, 2000), 236.

11. Since a new preface was added to the 1662 Book of Common Prayer, these essays were retained as "Concerning the Service of the Church," and "On Ceremonies, why some be abolished and some remain." For the texts, see Ketley, *Two Liturgies*, 17–19, 155–57.

he pointed out, have been beneficial. The keeping or omitting of a ceremony was a relatively minor thing in and of itself. But Cranmer could see how both traditionalism and radicalism were potential traps. The sheer volume and complexity of rites was one thing; a further problem was that many of them were "so dark, that they did more confound and darken, than declare and set forth Christ's benefits unto us." This spread of confusing and obscure rituals and rules had precisely the opposite effect that ought to be desired by any Christian church, for "Christ's Gospel is not a ceremonial law ... but it is a religion to serve God, not in the bondage of the figure or shadow, but in the freedom of the spirit." Cranmer was quite pragmatic, within his principle of decent order and discipline for the purpose of edification. He allowed for all kinds of ceremonies that might serve that end. But when that principle was obscured, he repudiated them. The abuse of these ceremonies by superstition and avarice was surely sufficient reason to reform the liturgical rules of the church, to the glory of God and the benefit of the congregation.

But Cranmer was not a radical, and he recognized here that his new rites would not be radical enough for some. He still retained some of the old ceremonies—it was of necessity to do so, he argued, since some order and discipline had to be maintained. With everything now explained in plain English, the ceremonies given in the book ought not to be a source of darkness and division among the people of God. To those who were hoping for a full-scale revision from scratch, he wrote:

> If they think much that any of the old do remain, and would rather have all devised anew: then such men (granting some ceremonies convenient to be had), surely where the old may be well used, there they cannot reasonably reprove the old (only for their age) without [revealing] their own folly. For in such a case they ought rather to have reverence unto them for their antiquity, if they will declare themselves to be more studious of unity and concord, than of innovations and newfangleness, which ... is always to be eschewed.

Perhaps conscious that he himself was accused of novelty by conservatives, Cranmer here denied that innovation was to be preferred simply for its own sake. Innovation and "newfangleness" were not virtuous in and of themselves for Cranmer. On the contrary, he was aiming at discipline and order, and could rightly point to the cacophony of liturgical forms in the previous era as a problem he had addressed.

By the same token, Cranmer clearly distinguished between the need for an order in the church established by human beings and practices upheld by the law of God. In matters of church order, he proved himself to be quite pragmatic, so long as unity, discipline, and edification were upheld. It was quite feasible, in his mind, for there to be different liturgical forms in different places and times, if properly justified. The church in each nation should have freedom to order its own ceremonies according to culture and circumstance.

> For we think it convenient that every country should use such ceremonies, as they shall think best to the setting forth of God's honour and glory, and to the reducing of the people to a most perfect and godly living, without error or superstition; and that they should put away other things, which from time to time they perceive to be most abused, as in men's ordinances it often chanceth diversely in diverse countries.

Cranmer claimed that he had simply excised those ceremonies which had fallen into the worst abuses. This was not necessarily a challenge to the ceremonies themselves. Ceremonies are not unchangeable as God's laws are. All this seems fairly mild and tolerable. However, we encounter in Cranmer's liberality here in 1549 the seeds of a controversy over public worship that would haunt the Church of England in the decades to come—between advocates of the "regulative" principle (only those things endorsed in Scripture ought to be allowed in church gatherings) and advocates of the "normative" principle (church ceremonies should not include things Scripture forbids).

If Cranmer had one overriding prayer for his liturgy, it would have been that worshipers should be "edified," a word he had gleaned from 1 Corinthians 14:5, where Paul speaks plainly of the need for intelligible language in the church's meetings so that the church will be "built up." As Cranmer wrote in a rubric to the "Preface," "All things shall be read and sung in the church, in the English tongue, to the end that the congregation may be thereby *edified*" (emphasis added).

The prayer books of 1549 and 1552 did not represent a completely fresh start from a blank slate. Nor were they as radical as some Continental liturgies were. As is often noted, Cranmer made use of material gleaned from existing services, as well as composing new elements himself. Nevertheless, the appearance of a vernacular liturgy was a radical statement in and of itself, however smooth the transition in terms of its content. Gordon Jeanes writes:

> From the point of view of the greater part of the English population, unexposed and unsympathetic to reform, both books were radical, and closer examination revealed a major theological shift which was more ambiguous in the first book and more obvious in the second. It would seem that Cranmer had a deliberate policy of reform by planned stages through the two books.[12]

From the appearance of the first Book of Common Prayer in 1549, then, it was apparent that a different theological construction of Christian worship was being offered to the English people. This is no more evident than in the way in which Cranmer invites the worshipers to confess their sins and hear absolution declared. The standard practice of auricular confession to a priest, in which the confessor carefully enumerated his or her sins and received a penitential task ("do penance"), had been replaced by a declaration of one's hatred of sin and a prayer for forgiveness.

Hence, the absolutions in the books of 1549 and 1552 employed the theology of justification by faith in their description of the for-

---

12. Jeanes, "Cranmer and Common Prayer," 26.

giveness of sins.[13] For example, the absolution from the Communion reads, "Almighty GOD, our heavenly Father, who of his great mercy, hath promised forgiveness of sins to all of them, which with hearty repentance and true faith turn unto him . . ."[14] The absolution added to the daily office in 1552 reads:

> He pardoneth and absolveth all them that truly repent, and unfeignedly believe his holy Gospel. Wherefore we beseech him to grant us true repentance and his holy Spirit, that those things may please him, which we do at this present, and that the rest of our life hereafter may be pure and holy.[15]

It is worth noting here that repentance itself is a gift from God *to* the believer. It is not described in any way as a tiny first step of the individual toward God. Even the heart of the believer needs the work of God to incline it in the right direction.

The expectation of an amended life replete with good works is seen in the prayer books as the fruit of this God-worked repentance: "And grant, O most merciful Father, for his sake, that we may hereafter live a godly, righteous and sober life, to the glory of thy holy name."[16]

Once more, we can see clearly that the prayer asks *God himself* to bring about the kind of changed life that is the evidence that the gospel has taken root. Justification and sanctification were not put on a separate theological footing—one being God's work, the other ours—but were on the same. Similarly, as the Ten Commandments were to be read out at the beginning of the Lord's Supper in the 1552 rendition, the congregation was invited to respond, "Lord, have mercy on us, and incline our hearts to keep this law."[17] It is true that in some parts of the liturgy of 1549, Cranmer left open the suggestion that the old system of individual confession and absolution was

---

13. Null, *Cranmer's Doctrine of Repentance*, 238.
14. Ketley, *Two Liturgies*, 91, 276.
15. Ketley, *Two Liturgies*, 219.
16. From the General Confession, added to the daily office in 1552. For the text, see Ketley, *Two Liturgies*, 219.
17. Ketley, *Two Liturgies*, 266.

still in place: "The Visitation of the Sick" even uses language reminiscent of the medieval *ego te absolvo* (I absolve you).[18] However, these formulae need to be understood against the backdrop of the prevailing theology of the whole book. Absolution is a declaration of the fact of the gospel word for the strengthening of the believer's faith, rather than an indication that the priest, by these words, actually of himself absolves the sinner from his or her sins.[19]

As on the Continent, the distinctive feature of the new liturgies was the prominent place they gave to the extensive reading of Scripture. In fact, Cranmer likely surpassed all other Reformation liturgists in this regard. Of course, more will be said about this shift in emphasis in chapter 3, which looks at preaching and the reading of Scripture. Not only did Cranmer append a detailed daily lectionary that allowed for Old Testament, Gospel, and Epistle readings; he also planned for the entire Psalter to be read through each month in its entirety. In addition to this, he made use of the words of Scripture in his prayers and other liturgical forms. It was, quite simply, a feast of Scripture; and no other order of public worship has ever really matched it. Cranmer's theological commitment to Scripture, not simply as the conveyer of information but also as the vehicle for the Spirit of God to do his work on the people, was very much in evidence.

The administration of the sacraments was another area in which there was significant and obvious change, reflecting a different theology of worship. As Jeanes puts it, for Cranmer, "worship expresses and nourishes relation to God but does not determine it: that is God's work alone."[20] This meant that the sacraments, as he understood them, were signs of the holy things of God but were not the holy things in themselves. Again, much more will be said about the sacraments in chapter 4, so I will confine myself to relatively few comments here.

---

18. Ketley, *Two Liturgies*, 138.
19. Null, *Cranmer's Doctrine of Repentance*, 240.
20. Jeanes, "Cranmer and Common Prayer," 30.

Cranmer's position, by the time of the Edwardian period, was in accord with the broadly "Reformed" (rather than Roman Catholic or Lutheran) position, which is to say that the sacraments work effectually only by faith. People can receive the outward token of the sacrament, but that sign remains an empty shell if they do not have faith. In the end, only the elect receive the grace to which the sacrament points. Jeanes explains, "Faith, as a gift of God, unites the outward sign and the inward grace, and the sacrament is then described as truly efficacious."[21] In the liturgies of 1549 and 1552, Cranmer appeared to say that all who received the sacraments also received the grace indicated by the sacraments, whether those persons were of the elect or not. Yet his (extensive) writings on the sacraments do not endorse that interpretation at all. It may be that Cranmer planned another, final revision of the liturgy, which would clarify things further.

The 1549 prayer book introduced its Communion service as "The Supper of the Lord and Holy Communion, Commonly called the Mass"—a somewhat ambivalent use of the old word *Mass*, simply recognizing that this was common parlance without actually endorsing its continued use. The word *altar* was still used; and the priestly vestments, such as the cope, were retained. By 1552 the word *Mass* had been removed. In November of 1550 the government ordered the removal of altars from churches and their replacement with wooden tables.

In the intervening years, two prominent Continental Reformers resident at the universities, Peter Martyr Vermigli and Martin Bucer, had offered extensive critiques of the previous prayer book. Prior to the publication of the 1552 revision, there was a dispute about whether the congregation should receive Communion kneeling or seated—on the basis that kneeling might indicate a veneration of the sacrament itself. In the final analysis, kneeling was the posture endorsed by the book, but the "Black Rubric" was added as an appendix.[22] This rubric explained what kneeling meant in the

---

21. Jeanes, "Cranmer and Common Prayer," 30.
22. For the text, see Ketley, *Two Liturgies*, 283.

minds of the composers of the prayer book. It explicitly denied that there was in the bread and wine any "real and essential presence there being of Christ's natural flesh and blood." In fact, quite the opposite was declared to be the case: the elements "remain still in their very natural substances, and therefore may not be adored, for that were Idolatry to be abhorred of all faithful Christians." Christ's body is in heaven, not on the table being sacrificed again. As if to underscore this point, Cranmer emphasized it in the service. The only sacrifice was the one already made, that of Christ on the cross—and this was "a full, perfect, and sufficient sacrifice, oblation and satisfaction, for the sins of the whole world."[23]

The twentieth-century liturgical scholar Dom Gregory Dix said of the 1552 Book of Common Prayer that it was "the only effective attempt ever made to give liturgical expression to the doctrine of 'justification by faith alone.'"[24] He no doubt overstated the extent to which Cranmer's theology was diluted in the revisions of 1559 and 1662. Nevertheless, the 1552 book was the high-water mark of the Cranmerian program for the renovation of the worship of the English people according to the tenets of the evangelical gospel. Sadly, it did not have a long provenance, since Edward VI promptly died in 1553, leaving his Roman Catholic sister, Mary, on the throne.

The Elizabethan Settlement and Its Aftermath

In his recent work *Anglican Theology*, Mark Chapman writes that "conflict is the normal state of 'Anglican' theology through history."[25] It has become somewhat of a lazy but intellectually cute habit (which Chapman himself deplores) in contemporary times to view this conflict as a good thing in itself, as a kind of Hegelian struggle that is of the *essence* of the church; or that *via media* solutions to these fierce debates are a sort of stable point from which to

23. Ketley, *Two Liturgies*, 88, 279.
24. Gregory Dix, *The Shape of the Liturgy*, 2nd ed. (London: Continuum, 2001), 672.
25. Mark D. Chapman, *Anglican Theology* (London: T&T Clark, 2012), 7.

comprehend the whole church. Yet, the fact that conflict is "normal" in the sense of common or ongoing (a description) doesn't make it a *norm* (a prescription, an ideal). The Elizabethan period was one such period in which struggle and conflict in church affairs repeatedly erupted. The conflict was in part due to Elizabeth's own knife-edge political situation and in part due to her own distaste for radicalism. Historically, we should agree with Chapman, I think, when he writes, "Perhaps the best way of conceiving the English Reformation is of a Reformation halted in progress, with many loose ends, not least in Church order."[26] Compromise is not beautiful in and of itself.

What is not in doubt, however, is that in the Elizabethan era, the Church of England was decidedly a *Reformed* church. It was not uniformly *Calvinist* but drew its influences from a broader group of Reformed thinkers, including Heinrich Bullinger; but it was certainly not clandestinely traditionalist Catholic, or even Lutheran, in its theology and worship. The reign of Queen Mary had led to the exile of many of the more Reformed church leaders and theologians to the Continent *en masse*; and these men settled for the duration in the great centers of Reformed Europe—Geneva and Strasbourg in particular. During this time, they became, for the most part, more radically Protestant than before. They witnessed how Calvin and Beza operated in Geneva in what was essentially a theocracy. They had time to think and write. One group even worked on the translation that would become the Geneva Bible, for more than eighty years the Bible of choice for the English people.[27]

For her part, the new queen stood now atop the slippery scaffold of power; and she knew just how precarious her position was. While she skillfully ensured that no one was in any doubt that England was a Protestant nation—rushing through her Acts

---

26. Chapman, *Anglican Theology*, 15.
27. See Michael Jensen, "'Simply' Reading the Geneva Bible: The Geneva Bible and Its Readers," *Literature and Theology* 9, no. 1 (1995): 30–45.

of Uniformity and Supremacy (1559) and appointing Protestant advisors—she also made it quite clear that she was not a supporter of the radicalism emerging from Geneva and the other Continental centers. While the prayer book of 1552 was retained, it was also altered: the Black Rubric was excised, and the 1549 words of administration ("the body of our Lord Jesus Christ") combined with the 1552 words ("Take and eat this in remembrance") to form a decidedly more ambiguous text. Elizabeth was not—adamantly not—in favor of Presbyterian church polity. Likewise, she would not endorse the wholesale removal of the surplice and, in fact, was pleased to see the return of the cope, alb, and stole. She was known not to favor lengthy sermons or the thought that there were unlicensed preaching groups in operation around the country. This set her and many of her bishops at odds with the group somewhat anachronistically known as the Puritans.

For our purposes here, we can see the Elizabethan period as one in which the essential elements of Cranmer's theological framework were not in dispute. The supreme authority of Scripture and the doctrine of justification by faith were by now assumed rather than debated. Nor was the priority of the electing grace of God the controversial point it would later become in the Stuart era. The dispute was now about how these two fundamental points ought to be related to the corporate worship of the church. Would Cranmer's pragmatism and flexibility be maintained? Or would a new rigorism after the style of Geneva win out? Did the theology of the Reformation in fact *demand* the regulative principle—and the end of all clerical vestments, all ornaments of any kind, and the suspicion of the symbolic?

The growing controversy over clerical vestments was an interesting test case. For some on the Puritan side, even the wearing of the surplice was indicative of priestcraft—a view of worship at odds with the evangelical gospel. Some bishops allowed a diversity of practice and even protected ministers who didn't wear vestments. However, in 1564, Archbishop Parker insisted on the wearing of the surplice in the case of two Oxford clerics who were refusing to conform. The controversy escalated to the point where, by 1566, Parker had to issue a directive, the "Advertisements," in which he insisted on the right of the queen to order the English church in doctrine and worship. The nonconformists wanted the freedom for total conformity to the word of God in all things, holding that there were no "things indifferent." On the establishment side, the bishops (and, of course, the queen) were happy to grant that some of these issues were not matters upon which Scripture had a view either way, but once a national church had decided on a specific course of action in one of these indifferent matters, then obedience to the law was the supreme concern. The fissure opened up by this dispute would only widen. The prominent Puritan theologian Thomas Cartwright of Cambridge, for example, who with much vigor argued for continued reform in the Elizabethan church, increasingly found himself out of favor with the national church and its leadership; and yet he was able to gather a significant following.

Richard Hooker is often seen as the doyen of Elizabethan theologians; yet his work was barely recognized in his own time (though he was praised by the queen and encouraged by Archbishop Whitgift). Because he has become such a landmark theologian in the later history of Anglican theological controversy, it is often easy to forget that Hooker was an adamant Protestant, zealous in his opposition to the pope; and in his soteriology, an exponent of justification by faith. Yet he wished to defend the Elizabethan Settlement against the Puritan party. In *The Laws of Ecclesiastical Polity*, he outlined in massive and solemn detail the way in which church government and worship ought to be arranged—with regard first and supremely to Scripture, but, where Scripture is silent, with regard to reason and tradition. This was essentially a riposte to the regulative principle espoused by men like Thomas Cartwright and William Perkins.

This is not the place for a detailed exposition of Hooker and his influence on later Anglicanism (which was immense by all accounts); suffice it for now to say that on worship, Hooker understood well the flexibility intended by Cranmer in the Book of Common Prayer. That is, he saw that rites and ceremonies of the church need not be expressly commanded in Scripture so long as everything was edifying. Vestments, for example, need not be seen as signs of compromise with the papacy but could be regarded simply as the expression of a due order, if commanded by the law of the land. Hooker saw ceremonies as valuable because they expressed continuity with the past. However, for Hooker the sermon had a less central place in the worship of the church, with the result that, as Diarmaid MacCulloch writes: "It was not surprising that with such preoccupations, Hooker was led towards increasing emphasis on the sacrament of the eucharist and its central place in the scheme of salvation; there could be no better expression of his ideal of the Church as a worshiping community."[28]

At the same time, the reform of the English liturgy did not seem to impact the cathedrals and college chapels in the same way that it did the parish churches. Choirs flourished still in these places and enjoyed the sponsorship of wealthy (and royal) patrons. Mac-Culloch opines, "The cathedral tradition thus came through what might have seemed unpromising Elizabethan years to reveal the potential for liturgical splendor in Cranmer's Book of Common Prayer (a development which, almost certainly, he would not have welcomed)."[29] In this development, and in the writings of Hooker, we see something of the uneasy compromise that came to be characteristic of the Church of England at worship. The intentions of the chief liturgist, Thomas Cranmer, were for some now a moot point. His attempt at a gradual reform of the worship of the English people in the direction of a more Reformed theology was diverted

---

28. Diarmaid MacCulloch, *The Later Reformation in England, 1547–1603*, 2nd ed. (Basingstoke: Palgrave, 2001), 84.

29. MacCulloch, *Later Reformation in England*, 80.

in the direction of an at times completely different, even inimical, theological outlook.

Reformation Anglican Worship Today

We have seen from this investigation of the worship practices in the English church during the Reformation that they were grounded in a specific set of theological convictions about (a) how human beings come to know God in the gospel of the Lord Jesus Christ and (b) how gatherings of believers ought to be ordered.

First, Cranmer was convinced that the European Reformation was essentially right in declaring that *the grace of God in Jesus Christ is the fundamental basis for an authentic Christian form of worship.* Out of the wellspring of grace came the material principle of the gospel, namely, the cross of Jesus Christ as a supply of mercy for a helpless and hopeless humanity before God. Christians could speak of having encountered God only because he had first encountered them. They could talk rightly of their worship of God only as a response of sheer gratitude to his grace. If human beings are justified only by faith in the gospel of divine grace, then they can come to know God only as those first known by him and to love God only as those first loved by him. If their lips were to show forth his praise, it was only because God had opened them.

Second, the formal principle by which the believer encountered this grace of God was that of *Holy Scripture*, the supreme authority for the church and sufficient in itself to describe and effect a person's salvation. It not only conveyed the data for salvation; *Scripture was the instrument of God's Holy Spirit to save human beings.* The Bible showed them their dire need for divine help; through its words, the Spirit of God turned them back to God in repentance; and by faith in its promises, believers received the blessings of God.

The worship of the English church was thus ordered by these principles to effect four outcomes. First, it was meant to edify those who took part in it. It was not to distract or detract from the adoration of Christ by those who attended. Second, it was meant to inspire in worshipers all manner of holy affections toward God, provoking them to pursue a life of honorable good works. Third, the worship of the English people was designed to have an impact on the society in which it took place. The prayer book was a political document, quite literally, in the sense that it served the ends of the monarchy, but also in that it was an attempt to shape a Christian society. It offered prayers for the monarch; but it also invited prayers to the almighty God, ruler of all rulers, to whom even the ruler was subject. By offering a single form of service in a single, unified form of the English language, the prayer book itself, for good or ill, offered a kind of coherence to the notion of England itself.[30] Fourth, it was a missionary document. Cranmer was under no illusions. His liturgy would have to convey the gospel message of grace as clearly as possible, because those who gathered to worship were not necessarily those who could be counted as among the godly. The church on earth was always a mixed rather than a pure gathering. It included (at least in theory) all citizens. And so, Jesus Christ needed to be the center of every gathering, in the hope that those who attended might hear and be saved.

Around these solid principles and outcomes was the worship of the Church of England organized, and they should be seen as its hallmarks. The Book of Common Prayer was never intended to be a book for all time and every place. It was designed to convey these principles to the England of the sixteenth century—an England in which Reformation theology had not yet taken hold. One of the tragedies of the history of the Church of England and indeed the wider communion is the way in which the outward form of the prayer book has been stubbornly retained long after its theology has been forgotten or even openly derided. The task for the Anglican Church of the twenty-first century is to find ways in which the timeless and universal theological principles of the Reformation era can find a timely and particular expression.

---

30. The Prayer Book Revolt of 1549 in Cornwall and Devon was at least in part prompted by resentment at the introduction of an English book for use in Cornish-speaking areas.

CHAPTER 3

Reading and Preaching the Scriptures

For preaching of the gospel is one of God's plough-works,
and the preacher is one of God's ploughmen.

Hugh Latimer, sermon, St Paul's Church, London, January
18, 1548[1]

Bishop Hugh Latimer (ca. 1492–1555) once protested: "How then
hath it happened that we have had so many hundred years so many
unpreaching prelates, lording loiterers, and idle ministers?"[2] Nevertheless, there certainly was preaching in the English church before the Reformation. There was even something of a revival of the
practice under the influence of humanist intellectuals like Erasmus
of Rotterdam and master preachers like Bishop John Fisher. But
the Reformation represented a theological shift that involved an
entirely different way of thinking about the word of God. Famously,
of course, this led to the creation of the English Bible and a liturgy
directing that it be read aloud in church. In turn, this also meant

---

1. Quoted in George Elwes Corrie, ed., *Sermons by Hugh Latimer* (Cambridge: Parker
Society, 1844), 60.
2. Corrie, *Sermons by Hugh Latimer*, 65.

that preaching and the preacher would come to have an entirely new—and central—significance for Reformation Anglicanism.[3]

As in so many other literary endeavors, the sixteenth century represented the high-water mark of sermon making in the English church. However, it might not be unfair to say that, in many places today, preaching is discounted. In some Anglican parishes, the sermon has shriveled to a perfunctory few minutes and has become, instead of a proclamation of the word of God, a mere moral rumination or a piece of self-help or the ponderous giving of the preacher's opinion, a kind of Sunday oral version of Saturday's newspaper column. Sad to say, Anglican preaching has become in popular culture a standing object of derision. One thinks of comedian Peter Cook's famous lampoon in the film *The Princess Bride,* or of Rowan Atkinson in *Four Weddings and a Funeral.*

The task for this chapter is to account for the centrality of reading and preaching Scripture in the Reformation Anglican conception of Christian worship, both corporate and individual. Once again, though, I must insist that my task is not primarily historical. The Reformation Anglican insistence on the centrality of the vernacular Scripture and its exposition by qualified preachers remains vital to the health of churches in the contemporary world. It is my hope that we will catch something of the spirit that animated the evangelical Reformers, not simply from antiquarian interest, but because it stemmed from a profound rediscovery of a truly biblical faith.

We will begin in conversation with a sermon on preaching by the English Reformation's most renowned preacher, Bishop Hugh Latimer. Then we will turn from there to see how Cranmer cemented the new doctrine of Scripture in the architecture of the church's corporate worship. Then, aided by one of the twentieth century's greatest Anglican pastor-preachers, John Stott, we will examine the basic theological convictions that give such prominence to the

---

3. This chapter is an expansion of Michael Jensen, "The Reformation of the Pulpit," *Credo* 7, no. 2 (2018), https://credomag.com/article/the-reformation-of-the-pulpit/.

preaching of the word. Stott's own ministry was a great model of the Reformation Anglican theology of Scripture transposed into another era, which in turn is a great model for the present day.

Hugh Latimer's Plough

Of the three leading English Reformers burned at the stake in Oxford under Queen Mary, it is easiest to imagine Hugh Latimer as the one least capable of compromise—the one who was most overtly evangelical in his preaching and who disdained the idea of reining himself in when the political tide turned against him. Latimer was, with Thomas Bilney and Robert Barnes, part of the group of Reformers that gathered at the White Horse Tavern in Cambridge in the 1520s. By 1535 he had been elevated to the see of Worcester and there began preaching an uncompromising program of reform. He was not able to stay out of trouble, however, and found himself imprisoned at the Tower of London in 1539 for his opposition to Henry's Six Articles. Once Edward VI had ascended to the throne in 1547, Latimer became court preacher, and his evangelical views could find their full expression in his preaching to the court and the Parliament.

The "Sermon of the Plough" of 1548,[4] on a portion of Romans 15:4 ("Whatever was written in former days was written for our instruction"), was delivered "in the shrouds" at St Paul's, which was an apparently sheltered area in the square outside the cathedral. The customary open-air sermons at St Paul's Cross were shifted to the shrouds in unfriendly weather conditions—which must have prevailed on the January day on which this sermon was preached. It was apparently part of a series of which this is the only extant sermon. In it, Latimer outlines his vision for the preaching ministry in the newly evangelical Church of England by means of the strikingly everyday image of the plough. He says, "I shall tell you who be the ploughers."[5]

---

4. Corrie, *Sermons by Hugh Latimer*, 59–78.
5. Corrie, *Sermons by Hugh Latimer*, 59.

Thus Latimer says, "Preaching of the gospel is one of God's plough-works, and the preacher is one of God's ploughmen."[6] He sources this agricultural metaphor in the parable of the sower—the seed being, in Jesus's story, "the Word." The congregation is God's field, in which the ploughman/preacher is set to work—not (and Latimer makes a point of this) the monk in his cloister. Thus he takes as his theme the diligent preaching of the word of God by the preacher in the congregation.

It is a vivid and earthy image—and deliberately so. Latimer feels compelled to draw attention to the possibility of this giving offense to some on account of its banality; but by the same token, he is quite proud of its ordinariness. It is a metaphor drawn from the everyday world of his hearers, matching the directness and plainness of his language, and reflecting as well his theology of the word of God—that it is in the words of ordinary language that God is pleased to speak.

As Latimer explains, the ploughman image is effective because the ploughman is in demand for his labor in all seasons of the year. The preacher of the word has different tasks to attend to if he is to be diligent: First, he has to plant the word and then cultivate it in his hearers: "He hath first a busy work to bring his parishioners to a right faith . . . and not a swerving faith; but to a faith that embraceth Christ, and trusteth to his merits; a lively faith, a justifying faith; a faith that maketh a man righteous, without respect of works."[7] In this we find the nexus between the Reformation doctrine of Scripture and the Reformation doctrine of justification. If a person is to be justified by faith, then the preaching of the word of God is necessary, since "faith comes from hearing" (Rom. 10:17); and this faith, by God's grace in Christ, is what enables sinful human beings to receive the gift of justification. That favorite Reformation phrase "a lively faith" is used: the faith that the preacher seeks to cultivate in his hearers is the faith that enlivens by the power of the Spirit as it draws the believer to the risen Christ.

---

6. Corrie, *Sermons by Hugh Latimer*, 60.
7. Corrie, *Sermons by Hugh Latimer*, 61.

Second, the people of God need to be confirmed in that right faith: to be disciplined by the law and comforted by the gospel, to be exhorted and rebuked. Changing his image, Latimer speaks of the preaching as "meat," namely, that which is in constant need for a solid diet. Therefore, the preacher ought to be diligent in all seasons.

The key role that preaching has in the soteriological system of the evangelical Reformers means that the preacher has a particular and extraordinary calling, and a responsibility to match. For too long, in Latimer's view, England has been subject to "unpreaching prelates." Furthermore, like unploughed ground, the land of England is spiritually unprepared for the seed, not yet "ripe to be ploughed." In particular, Latimer contrasts the "lording" of the clergy in pre-Reformation times with the new calling that they have, to preach. Plough work is not for those who would lord it over others: "Lords will ill go to plough."[8] Instead, those whose duty it is to feed the people have given themselves to all kinds of recreations, even though without the provision of the preached word of God the people will be lacking in spiritual sustenance (just as a ploughman's dedication to his task is necessary for the people to be fed): "For as the body wasteth and consumeth away for lack of bodily meat, so doth the soul pine away for the default of ghostly meat."[9] The priestly calling is to preach, and not to do some other thing, however noble, such as be comptroller of the mint.[10] The importance of this, for Latimer, is underscored by the ignorance of the young noblemen of England who should rather be "so brought up in knowledge of God, and in learning, that they may be able to execute offices in the commonweal."[11] For this to occur, those with a priestly calling and office need to attend to it without compromise, rather than busy themselves with matters of state.

---

8. Corrie, *Sermons by Hugh Latimer*, 66.
9. Corrie, *Sermons by Hugh Latimer*, 66.
10. Corrie, *Sermons by Hugh Latimer*, 67.
11. Corrie, *Sermons by Hugh Latimer*, 68–69.

The priestly office, of which preaching is the chief task, requires the full attention of a person.

The stakes are, for Latimer, extraordinarily high; for the most diligent "bishop" and "prelate" in England is unfortunately the devil himself. He is not inattentive to his task or absent from his diocese: "Oh that our prelates would be as diligent to sow the corn of good doctrine, as Satan is to sow cockle and darnel!"[12] The devil's mission is "to evacuate the cross of Christ" by adding the Mass to it as an extra sacrificial act.[13] Here we can see that the Reformation focus on the cross as the single center of a theology *sola gratia* is the gospel that needs diligent defense from its threatened dilution.

An interesting chain of reasoning is in play here. The preaching priest needs to be busy in affirming the gospel of the cross of Christ alone as the sacrifice for human sins against the alternate theology of the Mass and the view of the priesthood that attends it. There is no other bloody sacrifice, and that lone sacrifice of Christ is perpetual: "He is as fresh hanging on the cross now, to them that believe and trust in him, as he was fifteen hundred years ago, when he was crucified."[14] The view that the Mass is a sacrifice and that the priest is its sacrificer is, for Latimer, a piece of devilish idolatry. The channel of grace is not, therefore, the objects consumed in the Mass, nor is it the Communion vessels or the other accoutrements; it is the word of God, the gospel, preached by preachers and believed by those who listen and receive it.

In sum, we can observe two features of the Reformation description of preaching surfacing in this example of the preacher's art. The first is that, for Latimer, *the doctrine of justification by grace through faith alone is the basis for the new emphasis placed on preaching.* Grace is mediated, but not through the sacraments or through the church as an institution. It is mediated to the believer by God himself speaking in his word. The only way to

12. Corrie, *Sermons by Hugh Latimer*, 71.
13. Corrie, *Sermons by Hugh Latimer*, 72.
14. Corrie, *Sermons by Hugh Latimer*, 73.

receive this word is by means of the ears, by faith. "Faith comes from hearing." Thus, the word must be preached if it is to be heard. That is to say, the material and the formal principles at work in preaching are closely bound to one another—the place of preaching is a factor of what is to be preached. Sermons are needed for the edification of God's people, but they are more urgently needed for the purpose of leading people to salvation.

Second, *the ministry's chief responsibility is the preaching of the word and not something else.* Since the preached word is the divinely chosen means for the conversion and growth of God's people, the servant of God must preach! Preaching is, however, a task that takes hard work, courage, and persistence. This new emphasis for the ministers of the church is noteworthy because at one level it was contrary to one of the tenets of the evangelical Reformation—the priesthood of all believers. Why was there a need for a teaching office if in fact the Holy Spirit could walk directly into the lives of those who read the word for themselves? Did the Reformers not hold the Scripture to be clear, or "perspicuous"? Yet Cranmer and the later English Reformers took the lead from their Continental colleagues in emphasizing the need for an educated and trained preaching ministry. As Calvin wrote in the *Institutes*:

> We see that God, who might perfect his people in a moment, chooses not to bring them to manhood in any other way than by the education of the Church. We see the mode of doing it expressed; the preaching of celestial doctrine is committed to pastors. We see that all without exception are brought into the same order, that they may with meek and docile spirit allow themselves to be governed by teachers appointed for this purpose. . . . Hence it follows, that all who reject the spiritual food of the soul divinely offered to them by the hands of the Church, deserve to perish of hunger and famine. God inspires us with faith, but it is by the instrumentality of his gospel, as Paul reminds us, "Faith cometh by hearing" (Rom. 10:17). God reserves to himself the power of maintaining it, but it is by the preaching

of the gospel, as Paul also declares, that he brings it forth and unfolds it.[15]

Even though the Scriptures were the instrument of God by means of the Spirit for the softening of people's hearts, people still had to know and understand. The cognitive aspect of faith, though not faith in itself, is not bypassed by lively, justifying faith. On the contrary, having the Scriptures in the vernacular indicated that there was a new emphasis on understanding, and thus an educated—and diligent!—teaching ministry was to be an essential component of the evangelical Church of England. Susan Wabuda writes:

> The evangelical reformers retained the ancient ideal that preachers formed a special tier inside the greater body of Christendom, as administrators of the Word, to provide guidance in the correct interpretation of scripture. Godly ministers read the sacred page, and better: they taught, they explained, and they applied the text with more expertise and a greater measure of authority than any lay man or woman might be able to wield in the common assembly. Although no longer a mediator who sacrificed on behalf of the congregation, the preacher retained his position as the exemplar of sanctity. He was an intermediary still in the teaching of the Word. The preaching minister was a member of an elite who had self-consciously laid aside the popish affectations that had long obscured God's purpose. If permitting the laity to read the Bible in English was one of the greatest innovations of the Reformation, then it was balanced by the public teaching capacity which now became the greatest mandate of the clergy.[16]

The Emergence of the Evangelical Doctrine of Preaching

I have noted already that, prior to the Reformation, preaching was not in the abeyance suggested by Latimer's forceful rhetoric about

---

15. John Calvin, *Institutes of the Christian Religion*, ed. Henry Beveridge, trans. Henry Beveridge, rev. ed. (Peabody, MA: Hendrickson, 2008), 913 (4.1.5).

16. Susan Wabuda, *Preaching during the English Reformation* (Cambridge: Cambridge University Press, 2002), 66.

"unpreaching prelates." The late medieval church had in fact made significant provisions for regular preaching; and as part of priests' duties, it was expected that they would preach. The building of new pulpits in the fifteenth century surely indicates that at least some sermons were expected in church. Sermons were occasionally published, and preaching manuals circulated.[17]

The coming of European humanism to England heralded some new emphases in preaching, but built on the existing practices of preaching. Humanists like Erasmus of Rotterdam portended some of what was to come in the Reformation itself in that they were strong critics of church practices and wanted a return to a more biblical spirituality. Christianity, for Erasmus, was not a matter of the subtle distinctions of the medieval schoolmen but was a matter of attending to the plain teaching of the New Testament.[18] Nor was the essence of the faith to be found in the elaborate rituals of the church, since these were simply a matter of outward conduct. What humanism brought to the table instead was an interest in the human heart and its reformation. As Ashley Null writes, for Erasmus, "the heart of Christianity was a pragmatic programme of love in action which sprang from a scriptural understanding of the human condition and the virtues and vices pertaining to it."[19] For the Bible to have this role in the Christian life, it needed to be read and read well. And Erasmus was at the forefront of a movement for a new kind of exegesis of the text emphasizing philology and history rather than conformity to the systems of scholasticism.

For Erasmus and other humanist preachers like John Colet and John Fisher, preaching was vital, since it was a way to motivate people to live the virtuous life. Preaching was a means to move the affections by showing people the great love of God. Erasmus outlined this theology of preaching in his 1535 publication

---

17. Lucy Wooding, "From Tudor Humanism to Reformation Preaching," in *The Oxford Handbook of the Early Modern Sermon*, ed. Peter E. McCullough, Hugh Adlington, and Emma Rhatigan (Oxford: Oxford University Press, 2011), 330–34.
18. Ashley Null, *Thomas Cranmer's Doctrine of Repentance: Renewing the Power to Love* (Oxford: Oxford University Press, 2000), 86.
19. Null, *Cranmer's Doctrine of Repentance*, 86.

Ecclesiastes, a preaching manual. His hermeneutical principles were almost exactly those of the evangelical Reformers. He advised that Scripture ought to interpret Scripture; and that Scripture ought to be organized according to *loci communes* to facilitate this.[20]

Luther's disciple Philip Melanchthon adopted much of Erasmus's teaching in his work *Loci Communes Theologici* (1521). He outlined scriptural teaching under a series of headings, and he concurred that molding the affections of the congregation to produce a deeper love for God should be a goal of preachers. However, there was a significant difference between the anthropologies of the two authors. For Melanchthon, the affections of the human heart were held in bondage to concupiscence. As a result, the will was not free, and the capacity for reason did not allow the possibility of moderating and redirecting human behavior. John Donne would say almost a century later,

> Reason, your viceroy in me, me should defend,
> But is captiv'd, and proves weak or untrue.[21]

The human individual was turned on itself (*incurvatus in se*), twisted in its affections toward pursuing its own ends without hope of breaking the endemic pattern.

The only possibility for change was from an external, divine action. The Holy Spirit was to be the only hope for the moral life, if there was to be one at all. This implied the need not just for preaching but for preaching *of a particular content*: the gospel of Jesus Christ in whom sinners are freely justified. Null observes:

> When the good news of justification by faith was proclaimed, the Spirit assured believers of their salvation by working supernaturally through the power of God's word. This new confidence in God's gracious goodwill towards them reoriented their affec-

20. Ashley Null, "Official Tudor Homilies," in McCullough, Adlington, and Rhatigan, *Oxford Handbook of the Early Modern Sermon*, 353.
21. John Donne, "Batter My Heart," Holy Sonnet 14, lines 7–8.

tions, calming their turbulent hearts and inflaming in them a grateful love in return.[22]

This was clearly not simply a piece of theological nit-picking. It was intended to make an enormous pastoral and existential difference to those who heard it. When Cranmer came to organize the homilies that would be read in the churches of England in the 1540s, he gave them a distinctively evangelical shape in the light of the Melanchthonian doctrine. This indicated a distinct shift from the Erasmian humanist position. The homilies were designed to improve behavior and produce moral and social reform. But they did so as a consequence of the offer of the gospel of free grace in Christ and not as a means to attaining it. Cranmer's anthropology was certainly not Erasmian; and so his theology of justification could not be either. And this meant a distinct role for preaching and Scripture in the church, since the word was the chosen instrument of God to work his spiritual change in the lives of believers.

This pastoral theology of Holy Scripture is expounded in "A Fruitful Exhortation to the Reading and Knowledge of Holy Scripture," the first of the 1547 Book of Homilies. The homily shows the striking relationship we have already noted between form and content—Scripture is not simply the container of the data needed to know salvation but also its divinely ordained instrument: *"a sure, a constant, and a perpetual instrument of salvation."*[23] It is, naturally, the place to look for moral guidance; but it is, in the first place, the means by which we will come to a true knowledge of our desperate state before God: "In these books we may learn to know ourselves, how vile and miserable we be; and also to know God, how good he is of himself, and how he maketh us and all creatures partakers of his goodness."[24] The Bible is, for Cranmer, the means by which the supernatural operations of God are affected to turn the hearers to his will.

---

22. Null, "Official Tudor Homilies," 353.
23. John Griffiths, *Two Books of Homilies* (Oxford: Oxford University Press, 1859), 9.
24. Griffiths, *Two Books of Homilies*, 8.

For the Scripture of God is the heavenly meat of our souls: *the hearing and keeping of it* maketh us *blessed, sanctifieth* us, and maketh us holy: *it converteth our souls: it is a light lantern to our feet: it is a sure, a constant, and a perpetual instrument of salvation.* . . . They have power to turn through God's promise, and they be effectual through God's assistance; and being received in a faithful heart, they have ever an heavenly spiritual working in them.[25]

Even as Cranmer urges the activity of diligent reading on his hearers—something they are to do—he is simultaneously describing the gracious initiative of God in the whole process of turning the sinful heart around.

The comparison of Scripture to "meat" in the homily (and in Latimer's sermon) is a typical trope of the English Reformers, who spoke often of the Scripture as something to be tasted, chewed, and ingested by hearers. They were, as the 1549 Collect for the Second Sunday of Advent puts it, to "read, mark, learn, and inwardly digest" the Holy Scriptures.[26] Susan Wabuda notes, "For the reformers, a figural eating of the New Testament slowly displaced the traditional understanding of the testament of the sacrament of the altar."[27] The spiritual sustenance and nourishment that is found in Scripture is analogous to physical food. As "food," it has the nature of a blessing provided from above, on which the readers/hearers are dependent. The analogy has its own biblical basis in the episode of manna provided to the starving Israelites in the wilderness (Ex. 16:1–35); and in Jesus's feeding of the five thousand, recorded in all four Gospels (Matt. 14:13–21; Mark 6:31–44; Luke 9:12–17; John 6:1–14) as well as his saying "I am the bread of life," found in John's Gospel (6:35). It is interesting to note how the Reformers are willing to read this image figuratively, as opposed to the literalistic understanding of the medieval church. In this way,

---

25. Griffiths, *Two Books of Homilies*, 9.
26. Joseph Ketley, ed., *Two Liturgies . . . of Edward VI* (Cambridge: Parker Society, 1844), 42.
27. Wabuda, *Preaching during the English Reformation*, 85.

the "eating the word" trope in itself demonstrates the kind of "eating" that is to be done.

Scripture, Preaching, and Reformation Anglican Worship

> BLESSED Lord, which hast caused all holy Scriptures to
> be written for our learning: grant us that we may in such
> wise hear them, read, mark, learn, and inwardly digest
> them, that by patience and comfort of thy holy word,
> we may embrace, and ever hold fast the blessed hope of
> everlasting life, which thou hast given us in our Saviour
> Jesus Christ.[28]
>
> The Book of Common Prayer, 1549

In his masterful book *The Later Reformation in England, 1547–1603*, Diarmaid MacCulloch writes:

> [The Reformers] insisted that the text should be available to all:
> it was the only road to faith in Christ, which was the only means
> of salvation. This central message of scripture must be ex-
> plained constantly to humankind, now poised starkly and with-
> out the benefit of purgatory between heaven and hell, and the
> chief medium for doing it must be the sermon. The devotional
> world which they sought to construct was thus dramatically
> simpler than the rich and untidy fabric of medieval Catholicism,
> and at its centre, in place of the sequence of actions and formal
> texts which made up the mass, was the apprehension of a set of
> ideas by the Christian believer, fortified by constant access to
> the Bible in reading or in sermons. The emphasis had shifted
> from object and actions to words.[29]

It remains to be seen how, given this shift in the doctrine of Scripture, Cranmer and the other English evangelicals constructed this "devotional world" in the corporate worship of the Church of

---

28. Ketley, *Two Liturgies*, 42.

29. Diarmaid MacCulloch, *The Later Reformation in England, 1547–1603*, 2nd ed. (Basing-stoke: Palgrave, 2001), 4–5.

England. Given that the word of God, and not rites of the church or holy objects, was held to be God's means to bring people to a saving repentance and faith, how would that shape the pattern and content of the new liturgy? What other innovations would be promoted in the service of this new theology?

Four policies in particular were pursued. First, Cranmer offered the English people a feast of Scripture in the English tongue in his Book of Common Prayer, such that the Scriptures could scarcely be avoided. Second, the translation and distribution of the Bible into English went from being a cloak and dagger activity to being a government policy. Third, the architecture of churches was altered to ensure both the clear reading of Scripture and the prominence of preaching. And fourth, Cranmer and later Reformers actively promoted and funded preaching as well as the education of preachers. This collection of policies was designed to ensure that whatever else one might say about Anglican worship thereafter, one would have to take note of the central place that the ministry of the word, read and preached, had in it.

Scripture and the Book of Common Prayer. An obviously prominent feature of the Book of Common Prayer published first in 1549 is the place it gives to the regular reading of the vernacular Scriptures. It has been shown many times in the vast literature on the creation of the Book of Common Prayer that Cranmer used an array of preexisting materials to compile his book, including the old Sarum rite. But what was strikingly new about the prayer book was that it was in English—a clear signal to the congregations of the land that they were actually being addressed in the new services.

In his preface to the 1549 book, Cranmer wrote,

> And moreover, whereas St Paul would have such language spoken to the people in the church, as they might understand and have profit by hearing the same; the service in this Church of England (these many years) hath been read in Latin to the people, which they understood not; so that they have heard with

their ears only; and their hearts, spirit, and mind, have not been edified thereby.[30]

The new, English words of the prayer book would penetrate into the very souls of the hearers via the portal of the ears. Without bare cognition, at the very least, edification is impossible. The necessity for verbal intelligibility is paramount.

The introduction of a lectionary of set readings to go with the book was, as Cranmer explained, a revival of the practice of the ancient fathers. But something of the evangelical doctrine of Scripture was indicated by it too. Joseph Ketley explained, "Here is drawn out a Kalendar . . . which is plain and easy to be understanded; wherein (so much as may be) the reading of holy Scripture is so set forth, that all things shall be done in order, without breaking one piece thereof from another."[31] In short, Cranmer's endeavor was to present Scripture to the people entire, with as little selectivity and editing as possible, so that they would be able to hear the Bible *as a whole* and would be able to see how interconnected the Bible is. Scripture, thereby, would be able to interpret Scripture. Cranmer ensured that the New Testament would be read through three times annually, and the Old Testament once—with a special place for the Psalms, which would be read through every month.

As Hughes Oliphant Old writes, "In England the reshaping of the lectionary found in *The Book of Common Prayer* was a genuine reformation of the ministry of the Word."[32] The new prayer book with its lectionary was a deliberate inculcation of the Scriptures understood to be God's instrument for the salvation of men and women. During the Elizabethan period, Richard Hooker would write:

> The end of the Word of God is *to save*, and therefore we term it *the word of life*. The way for all men to be saved is by the

---

30. Ketley, *Two Liturgies*, 17–18.
31. Ketley, *Two Liturgies*, 18.
32. Hughes Oliphant Old, *The Age of the Reformation*, vol. 4, in *The Reading and Preaching of the Scriptures in the Worship of the Christian Church*, 7 vols. (Grand Rapids, MI: Eerdmans, 2002), 149.

knowledge of that truth which the word hath taught. . . . To this end the word of God no otherwise serveth than only in the nature of a doctrinal instrument. It saveth because it maketh "wise to salvation." (II Tim. 2:15)[33]

Two practical considerations were also relevant. In the first place, Cranmer could not guarantee that in many or even most parishes there would be an educated clergyman who could make informed decisions about the public reading of Scripture. Second, it would not be until the 1560s that English Bibles became freely available to the general public for their own private reading. The liturgy would have to be the chief source of faith formation.[34]

The translation of the Bible into the vernacular for reading in church. The humanists and the evangelicals shared the deep desire to see the Scriptures translated into the vernacular languages of Europe, since they both believed that the intellect was not to be bypassed in the binding of a person to God. The translation of the Bible into English had been given its impetus by the remarkable and courageous work of William Tyndale, who was martyred by the henchmen of Henry VIII for his pains in 1536. Nevertheless, Tyndale's work was the basis of the first complete official English Bible, the Great Bible, which was guided to production by Miles Coverdale in 1539.[35] The "Great" Bible (sometimes also called the "Chained" Bible) was so-called because of its great size and because it was frequently chained in place to prevent its theft. It was clearly a Bible designed for reading in the context of the liturgy.

At the same time, as Cranmer's preface to the second edition of the Great Bible (1540) makes clear, he envisaged the English Bible playing a central role in the individual spirituality of the English

---

33. John Keble, ed., *The Works of . . . Richard Hooker*, 7th ed., 3 vols. (Oxford: Clarendon, 1888), 2:85 (*Laws of Ecclesiastical Polity*, 5.21.3).

34. Old, *Age of the Reformation*, 159.

35. Note, however, that on his own initiative John Rogers compiled and printed an earlier complete version under the pseudonym "Thomas Matthew" (hence its name, "Matthew's Bible"), the sale of which the government approved in England, at Cranmer's request, as an interim measure in 1537.

people, in the home and at labor as much as in church services. He adopted his theme from a sermon by John Chrysostom:

> Therefore sayth he there, "My common usage is to give you warning before, what matter I intend after to entreat upon, that you yourselves, in the mean days, may take the book in hand, read, weigh, and perceive the sum and effect of the matter, and mark what hath been declared, and what remaineth yet to be declared: so that thereby your mind may be the more furnished to hear the rest that shall be said. And that I exhort you," saith he, "and ever have and will exhort you, that you not only here in the church give ear to that that is said by the preacher; but that also, when ye be at home in your houses, ye apply yourselves, from time to time, to the reading of holy Scriptures."[36]

The subsequent history of the English Bible is a fascinating tussle between individual and public readers. Cranmer is clear in his preface that while all people should have access to the Scriptures in their own language, and should be encouraged to meditate upon them constantly, not all readers are likewise skilled, competent, and authoritative. In this way, he hoped to establish a line of authority—based on reasonableness—between the church's Bible reading practices and the individual believer's Bible reading. The publication of the cheap and popular Geneva Bible in 1560—before any revision of the Great Bible could be made—took the reading of the Bible in English out of the hands of the authorities. Despite the publication of the Bishops' Bible in 1568, it was not until the 1660s that the Bible an English man or woman heard read in church was the same as the Bible he or she read at home.[37]

A new design for church buildings and furniture. Having a comprehensive program of Bible reading at the center of the Church of

---

36. Henry Jenkyns, ed., *The Remains of Thomas Cranmer*, 4 vols. (Oxford: Oxford University Press, 1833), 2:106, quoting from John Chrysostom, *De Lazaro*, sermon 3.
37. For more on the Geneva Bible and its readers, see Michael Jensen, "'Simply' Reading the Geneva Bible: The Geneva Bible and Its Readers," *Literature and Theology* 9, no. 1 (1995): 30–45.

England's worship might seem enough. Was there any need to add to this emphasis on preaching? And, certainly, if the laity could now read the Bible, was there any reason for keeping a separate, pulpiteering elite? We have already seen how the Reformation doctrine of the word of God required not simply the reading of the word but also the *preaching* of the word. The new liturgy did not, however, find as prominent a place for preaching as had been seen in Continental services. Indeed, by the time of Richard Hooker, a reaction against sermons was underway, with Hooker— who held the Cranmerian view that the Scripture was the divine instrument for a saving knowledge of the truth—arguing against the Puritans that "*sermons* are not *the only preaching* which doth save souls."[38]

It certainly crossed the minds of some that the elaborate pulpits of the English churches should disappear as reflective of the trappings of popery. With characteristic vigor, Latimer argued that the sermon could be delivered from any place at all, even from the back of a horse.[39] But this view did not prevail. As we have already noted, in line with their Continental colleagues, the evangelical Reformers of England were not prepared to let go of the notion of a magisterial rank of believers whose better-educated opinions—while not infallible—were of more weight than others. As Wabuda puts it, "Preaching still required a measure of inspiration that even the most careful readers lacked."[40]

The interior design of English churches came to reflect this teaching. The point was to make *hearing*, and not seeing, the main activity. The pulpit, once associated with the high altar, was now moved into the body of the church where it could be more readily seen and the words coming from it more clearly heard. The preacher was elevated above the people; sometimes *far* above the people. The seventeenth century introduced into many churches a

---

38. Keble, *Works of Hooker*, 2:86 (*Laws of Ecclesiastical Polity*, 5.21.4).
39. Wabuda, *Preaching during the English Reformation*, 105.
40. Wabuda, *Preaching during the English Reformation*, 106.

clear hierarchy of platforms. The reading desk was the place from which the clerk read the Psalms and helped the congregation with their responses. Higher than this was the place from which the prayers were recited by the minister. But higher still was the pulpit for preaching. Indeed, these were in some instances combined into a single "three-decker" pulpit, which became quite a common feature of Anglican churches during the eighteenth century. This imposing piece of ecclesiastical furnishing clearly communicated the presence and necessity of preaching, even when Scripture was to be read.[41]

English churches from the Reformation until the nineteenth century were designed chiefly as auditoriums. The practice of reading Scripture aloud and of preaching sermons necessitated this design, which held sway until the Gothic Revival—itself a product of a particular (and very different) theology of worship.

The promotion of preaching and preachers. We have already noted that the evangelical Reformers saw preaching as the chief role of the ministry to which all other roles were subordinated. From the beginnings of the English Reformation on, Archbishop Cranmer had been aware of the need to promote effective evangelical preachers and to make provision for the training of a knowledgeable priesthood. Cranmer licensed preachers in a number of dioceses and nominated men for particular parishes in the hope that they would gain a more regional influence through their preaching.

The need was as obvious as it was pressing, all throughout the sixteenth century. MacCulloch writes, "For the first Reformers and for most of their Elizabethan successors, the ideal was for every church in the land to have provision for a sermon at all major acts of worship, and this demanded a huge redirection of effort within the ministry."[42]

---

41. James F. White, "Prayer Book Architecture," in *The Oxford Guide to the Book of Common Prayer: A Worldwide Survey*, ed. Charles C. Hefling and Cynthia L. Shattuck (Oxford: Oxford University Press, 2006), 108–9.

42. MacCulloch, *Later Reformation in England*, 96.

Though there were some short-term solutions, such as the ordination of older men, the long-term strategy pursued in the Elizabethan era was to improve the quality of the clergy—the requirements
for ordination were made more stringent, for example. By raising
the age at which one could be made a deacon to twenty-three years,
the time in which a man could undertake proper education prior to
ordination was expanded. As MacCulloch notes, by the 1620s re-
cruitment of clergy was almost entirely from university graduates.[43]

During the Elizabethan era tensions did, however, develop between the Puritan party, for whom a new weekly sermon was a
nonnegotiable, and the leaders of the church such as Archbishop
Whitgift, for whom catechizing rather than the liturgical act of
preaching was the priority. In order to make space for preaching,
the unofficial sponsorship of "lectureships" sprang up, especially
in market towns. These endowments created local preachers-
without-parishes. While this was not to the taste of many diocesan
hierarchies, and certainly was the focus of serious conflict in the
seventeenth century, there were cases in which this system of lectureships supplemented parish ministry quite successfully.[44]

These four strategies for implementing the Reformation theology
of the word in the worship of the church illustrate just how deep
the change of theological understanding ran in the minds of the
evangelical Reformers. Worship was not, as they saw it, the human
endeavor to please a distant deity. It was instead a response to a God
who speaks; and the word that the God who is Father, Son, and Holy
Spirit speaks is a word that is a declaration of his great offer of grace
and mercy toward sinners in Christ, who can thus approach him in
humble confidence.

---

43. MacCulloch, *Later Reformation in England*, 98.

44. MacCulloch, *Later Reformation in England*, 100. For more on Puritan lectureships, see
Paul S. Seaver, *The Puritan Lectureships: The Politics of Religious Dissent, 1560–1662* (Stanford, CA: Stanford University Press, 1970).

A Theology for Preaching, in Conversation with John Stott

Throughout this book my interest has not been to prove that my reading of historical Anglicanism is somehow more authentic than others'. This was the strategy (from another point of view) of the Oxford movement in the nineteenth century. And Mark Chapman, among others, writes about how historically dubious, to the point of dishonesty, this claim was:

> For many nineteenth-century writers, [Diarmaid MacCulloch] claimed, the Reformation simply 'did not happen', or if [it] did happen, 'it happened by accident rather than design or . . . was half-hearted and sought a middle way between Catholicism and Protestantism'. Such a myth lies behind the grandiose claim of some nineteenth-century figures who viewed Anglicanism as the English branch of the Church Catholic alongside—and perhaps even superior to—Roman Catholicism and Orthodoxy and quite distinct from the heresies of Continental Protestantism. While this is about as gross a distortion of history as it is possible to make, it was deeply influential on the perception and identity of Anglicanism, not least in its approach to theology, as well as in the closely related fields of liturgy and architecture.[45]

That there is a distinctly evangelical flavor in the theology and practice of worship introduced to the Reformation-era Church of England in its formularies and its other practices is really indisputable. And if we are to take the sixteenth century as a fulcrum point for Anglican theology and practice, then that is a significant point. But the more important question is rather *So what?* If this theology is itself simply mistaken, or a complete distortion of authentic biblical Christianity, then whether it is true to the sixteenth-century formularies of the Church of England or to the theological conviction of Thomas Cranmer is really beside the point.

---

45. Mark D. Chapman, *Anglican Theology* (London: T&T Clark, 2012), 2.

Having established that the preaching and reading of Scripture became the focal point of Reformation Anglican worship, we still need to ask whether that conviction is well-founded. To show that it is, I propose in this next section to take my lead from the doyen of evangelical Anglican preachers in the latter half of the twentieth century, sometime rector of All Souls, Langham Place, John Stott. Dr. Stott outlines his biblical and theological rationale for preaching in his 1982 book *I Believe in Preaching*.[46] There he helps his readers to see that the mandate for the centrality of preaching is founded on an interrelated series of theological convictions. I follow his outline with some small variations and my own expositions of the themes.

The God of Jesus Christ is a God who speaks. The basic theological principle for a theology of preaching is the claim that the Christian God is a God who reveals himself in speech. The idea of a chiefly verbal Christianity has come under renewed assault in the twentieth century. This of course resonates with apophatic tradition within Christianity,[47] and it is no accident that Jacques Derrida, Michel Foucault, and other postmodernists were attracted to the writings of the ancient apophatic theologian Pseudo-Dionysius. Words are too susceptible to becoming the instruments of power or spin; words are too slippery, too inexact, too imperfect an instrument; words are too limited to contain the transcendent Almighty. As Gregory of Nazianzus once prayed (Oration 40):

> You remain beyond the reach of speech.
> All that is thought stems from you,
> But you are beyond the power of thought.

---

46. John R. W. Stott, *I Believe in Preaching* (London: Hodder & Stoughton, 1982).

47. Apophatic, or negative, theology is a way of approaching God by recognizing how an infinite God is ultimately unknowable in his essence by finite human beings. Human conceptions of and even human language about God in himself are necessarily limited to approximations in their descriptions and, in the final analysis, remain inadequate to make God fully known. Therefore, God should be sought not by intellectual understanding but rather through a direct experience of him.

Archbishop Peter Carnley, former Anglican Primate of Australia, pointed out in his book *Reflections in Glass* that Christian theology must start from a core affirmation of the unknowability and sheer transcendence of God: "I particularly value . . . the basic theological truth that God, by definition, is an infinite mystery, an ineffable, transcendent reality. This means that by definition God is beyond all our finite images of him, and beyond all our attempts to express or describe him in finite human words."[48] However, that *via negativa* must be accompanied by a *via positiva*. The triune God is transcendent but has drawn near; he is unknowable but has made himself known. True Christian worship is never of a God unknown but of a God who speaks about himself to us. Do we have or do we not have a gospel, a message that originates from the divine? The contrast between the paganism of the Athenians and Paul's message in Acts 17:23 is apposite: "For as I passed along and observed the objects of your worship, I found also an altar with this inscription: 'To the unknown god.' What therefore you worship as unknown, this I proclaim to you." These are presumptuous words indeed if human words cannot meaningfully speak about the divine. And yet Paul is presenting his message not as another attempt fitfully to describe God from the human side but as the message of a decisive intervention from God in Christ Jesus, the crucified and risen Lord.

The sending of the Logos, God the Son, into the realm of women and men—the incarnation, in other words—is often described as the central theological theme of Anglicanism (to the point of cliché). The incarnation of the Son in the likeness of sinful flesh means that the enormous gulf between God and humanity has been overcome. It means that human flesh is an entirely possible dwelling place for divinity. It also means that human words are entirely possible as vehicles for divine self-communication. The ancient heresy of Gnosticism—which decried the flesh and emphasized the concealment of a mystery rather than its revelation—has been rejected as

---

48. Peter Carnley, *Reflections in Glass: Trends and Tensions in the Contemporary Anglican Church* (Pymble, NSW: HarperCollins, 2004), 27.

antihuman by Christians consistently since the time of Irenaeus. Body is not to be played off against the soul; nor is the intelligible to be played off against that which is beyond reason. Paul's preference for intelligible words over ecstatic tongues in the Christian meeting in 1 Corinthians 14 is instructive.

In the gospel of Jesus Christ, men and women are addressed by the God who creates with a word. This mustn't be understood reductionistically, of course, as if God could be contained or captured by human words. The prologue of John's Gospel sums this up well: "No one has ever seen God; the only God, who is at the Father's side, he has made him known" (1:18).

God is beyond us and our words. But we are not beyond him, and we are not beyond the sound of his voice. Nor is it beyond the people of God to pass on what we have heard God say. So the apostle Peter writes, "But you are a chosen race, a royal priesthood, a holy nation, a people for his own possession, that you may proclaim the excellencies of him who called you out of darkness into his marvelous light" (1 Pet. 2:9).

Those who have heard the call of God are commissioned to proclaim his works to the nations as a priestly duty. Just as Jesus himself came to proclaim a message of good news about himself— "the Spirit of the Lord is upon me, / because he has anointed me / to proclaim good news to the poor" (Luke 4:18)—so his apostles were commissioned to rehearse the life, death, resurrection, and glorious return of their Lord in the hearing of the nations. God, in other words, speaks: in human language, through human beings, to human beings.

The Bible is the word of God written. John Stott, reflecting on Article 20 of the Thirty-Nine Articles, writes: "'God's word written' is an excellent definition of Scripture."[49] This claim depends on the history, which Scripture itself records, of God's communicative activity with and toward people, culminating in the coming of

---

49. Stott, *I Believe in Preaching*, 96.

Jesus as God's unsurpassed Word. The writing down of the divine communication is itself an activity that Scripture describes, from the description of Moses recording the law in Deuteronomy (31:9) onward. By the lifetime of the Lord Jesus, it was quite clear that the theology of Scripture as the inspired word of the divine author speaking through human beings had become developed. Jesus himself is recorded as treating the written words of the Hebrew Scriptures as inspired by God. For him, Scripture was the authority to which he would appeal repeatedly to make sense of his own divinely ordained mission. In Mark 7:8–13, we find him contrasting the written law as "the commandment of God" with the merely human traditions of the Pharisees and teachers of the law.

Scripture records that, in Scripture, God still speaks. In Hebrews 3–4, for example, the author quotes the words of Psalm 95 (used so well by Cranmer in the prayer book):[50]

Today, if you hear his voice,
do not harden your hearts. (vv. 7–8)

In introducing the quotation, he uses the words "as the Holy Spirit says"—thereby indicating that the ancient written word is very much a present word, addressed to anyone who reads the letter. The seven letters to the seven churches in Revelation 2–3 contain the formula "he who has an ear to hear, let him hear what the Spirit says to the churches." The words of the letters are the words of the Spirit—in other words, divine words—and they are the words written for the benefit of any who read them.

It is the person of the Holy Spirit who is particularly associated with originally inspiring and, at the time, continuing to inspire the words of Holy Scripture as the living and active word of God. In other words, God himself is at work in his words. This of course is a specifically New Testament way of understanding the presence of God in the words of Scripture, but in Psalm 119,

---

50. Ketley, *Two Liturgies*, 29.

an extraordinary hymn to the written words, we see the author coming close to associating the person of YHWH with the text of the Torah. His delight in the written words is an act tantamount to worship:

> My soul is consumed with longing
>> for your rules at all times. (Ps. 119:20)

That means that the words of Scripture speak with the authority and power of the divine being—the Creator, Judge, and Redeemer. The words of Scripture are not, for the Christian, suggestions, ruminations, moving examples of human spirituality, or simply beautiful. The words, written by human beings and preserved through all the battering of history, stand as God's word to humankind. And they are powerful words, shaped for the purpose of redeeming people. That was a particular conviction of the Anglican Reformers: that the Holy Scripture contains "all that is necessary for salvation" (Article 6 of the Thirty-Nine Articles) and that it is powerful to accomplish that purpose.

Humanity's great need is to hear the voice of God. The devotion of the psalmist to the precepts and promises of God in Psalm 119 is instructive: the voice of God is what sustains him and nourishes him. Without the word of God, he cannot stand. When Jesus Christ matched wits with the devil in the wilderness, Jesus himself drew on the Scriptures (and, note, not some extraordinary virtue) as his means of surviving the trials put before him. He recalled especially that great exodus statement:

> Man shall not live by bread alone,
>> but by every word that comes from the mouth of God.
>>> (Matt. 4:4 citing Deut. 8:3)

We have already seen how the English Reformers delighted in the analogy between consuming food (usually "meat" for them) and reading the word of God. They were reflecting the long metaphorical association between the two ideas found on the pages of Scripture. The paradigmatic instance appears in the exodus period, when Israel's faith in the promises of God is sorely tested by hunger and thirst, and when he provides for them the manna from heaven—which in turn becomes a symbol for his word to them and their trust in him. The word of prophecy was seen as necessary in the later history of Israel to keep the nation alive. Consequently, Amos pronounced a terrible curse when he warned Israel that there would be a famine of divine communication:

> "Behold, the days are coming," declares the Lord GOD,
>   "when I will send a famine on the land—
> not a famine of bread, nor a thirst for water,
>   but of hearing the words of the LORD." (Amos 8:11)

This was a frightful judgment. Without the words of the Lord, Israel would lose its bearings and its identity—it would scarcely survive. The purpose of the people with whom God made the covenant would surely be lost if his voice could not be heard.

Humanity needs the word of God because otherwise we are spiritually in the dark. In the prologue to John's Gospel, John seems unconcerned about piling up his images and symbols so that they almost tumble over one another: "word," "light," "life." The Logos-word is "light": it provides illumination to people. And people need illumination because they are very much in the dark. That darkness is not simply ignorance: it is an ignorance that has a profoundly disturbing spiritual significance. Without the voice of God, human beings are living away from the source of life itself, and in the grip of a terrible pattern of self-destruction. Life without that life-giving voice is ultimately life without hope.

The Scriptures are, to recall again the words of Article 6, the book that contains all that a person needs to know for salvation—which is a person's greatest need. It is, in other words, an *evangelical* book first and foremost. The Bible is good news because it contains the good news that sinful human beings need the most; and it is the means by which God brings such people, through himself, to a saving encounter with him.

The church is a creature of God's word. The church is dependent for its being on the word of God. Like the creation itself, it is called into being by its Lord.[51] Without the gospel of the crucified and risen Son of God, the church is not a people—as Peter writes to the "aliens and exiles" scattered throughout the provinces of Asia Minor: "Once you were not a people, but now you are God's people; once you had not received mercy, but now you have received mercy" (1 Pet. 2:10).

It is, of course, a matter of simple historical fact that, as documents, the texts of the New Testament were written, collected, and recognized by believing Christians. Sometimes this activity was at an "official" or institutional level, though more often than not it was a rather haphazard process. That does not mean, however, that the church stands as an authority over the Scriptures. The whole dynamic of the biblical pattern of the *calling* of the people of God, from Abraham onward, invites us to see that, even when God uses human words as his instruments and involves human interpreters in receiving them, the initiative and the authority still remain with him. Stott writes:

> Throughout Scripture God is addressing his people, teaching them his way, and appealing to them both for his sake and for theirs to hear and heed his message. If it is true "that man does not live by bread alone, but that man lives by everything that proceeds out of the mouth of the Lord" . . . the same is true of the Church. God's people live and flourish only by believing and obeying his Word.[52]

The late Anglican theologian John Webster adds, "Very simply, the church alone is not competent to confer authority on Holy Scripture, any more than it is competent to be a speaking church

---

51. Stott, *I Believe in Preaching*, 109.
52. Stott, *I Believe in Preaching*, 110.

before it is a hearing church, or competent to give itself the mandate to be apostolic."[53] The ongoing vitality of the Christian church depends on the degree to which it recognizes the source of its very being and attends to this. It knows who it is as it recognizes its Master's voice; and that voice is heard as Scripture is read and preached.

The ministry is chiefly a ministry of the word. The apostles themselves were very careful to institute practices within church communities that would ensure that their teaching would be preserved. And chief among these was the creation of the offices of ministry by which some individuals are designated and authorized to maintain and transmit the "good deposit." The eldership that we see created in the Pastoral Epistles was very much intended for the service of the Christian community—not as an intermediary priesthood, but as a didactic pastorate. "It was and is a ministry of the Word," says Stott,[54] commenting on the Anglican ordinal.

Does this always mean *preaching* in the modern sense of the word? We ought to recognize that the sermon as we know it today does not exactly fit the New Testament vocabulary of teaching, preaching, prophesy, and exhortation. The sermon may involve all of these activities; and these activities may occur in formal or less formal settings—or even between two believers as one opens the Scriptures with another. Nevertheless, the traditional sermon is a recognition that the center of the church's worship is the act of listening to the speaking God.

Ministers of the word are ministers of *the word*—which means that they are not simply in the business of giving advice, or of pop psychology, or of drinking cups of tea. The tool of their trade is the Bible, since by serving it they serve the gospel of the Lord they have sworn to serve. This takes a certain set of gifts, a certain character, and a due diligence. They should be "able to teach" (2 Tim. 2:24). They should be "above reproach, the husband of one wife,

---

53. J. B. Webster, *Holy Scripture: A Dogmatic Sketch* (Cambridge: Cambridge University Press, 2003), 53.

54. Stott, *I Believe in Preaching*, 118.

sober-minded, self-controlled, respectable, hospitable . . . not a drunkard, not violent but gentle, not quarrelsome, not a lover of money" (1 Tim. 3:2). But the ministry of the word takes considerable labor in careful study of the Scriptures, so that the people of God might be "filled with the knowledge of God's will in all spiritual wisdom and understanding" (Col. 1:9).

That means that the caricature of Protestantism, that everyone does what is right in his or her own eyes as far as reading Scripture goes, ought to be wide of the mark, since a teaching eldership is inaugurated so as to prevent a hermeneutical cacophony. The Reformers of the Church of England were insistent, against the radical Anabaptist sects, that the learned had a responsibility to shepherd the unlearned. They readily acknowledged that though Scripture is "clear" in that the message of the gospel is plain to see for anyone who cares to look, there are obscure places in the text that need expert knowledge to understand rightly.[55]

The ministry of proclamation is not merely the giving of opinions or perspectives. It is a recital of God's word to human beings, and in this derivative sense may properly be called "the word of God." It therefore requires an attitude of fear and trembling from the one who would so preach. It asks for an unlearning of the hermeneutic of suspicion, which questions the validity and veracity of the biblical text, and instead demands that the proclaimer allow Scripture to form in him or her an attitude of receptive and humble listening. The pulpit in the Anglican church is not merely the preserve of the priest: it may be perfectly appropriate for a layperson to speak, as in fact happens frequently. But the pulpit ought to be guarded with some jealousy as the place from which the word of God is proclaimed and taught to the people of God.

---

55. Drawing on John Chrysostom's commentary on Philip and the Ethiopian eunuch (Acts 8:26–40), Cranmer himself made this point in the Homily on Scripture. Griffiths, *Two Books of Homilies*, 13–14.

These five convictions about the word of God underpin the evangelical practice of making the reading and preaching of Scripture central to the worship of the church. The word of God recorded in Scripture is the lifeblood of the church: which means that the church cannot do without hearing the Scriptures speak. No other practices of worship are as vital to its spiritual health.

The Future of Preaching in Anglican Worship

How, then, can the Anglican churches of today ensure that they are true to their Reformation roots? How can they—and this is more important, in fact—be true to their identity as creatures of the gospel word? There is no more pressing question for a church in this or any other era. But we should not think that the answer is especially complicated, and it is this: The Bible must not be silent in the churches. It must be allowed to have its say. To that end, Reformation Anglican churches should not neglect the careful, clear, and comprehensive reading of the Scriptures in corporate worship; nor should they neglect preaching. Indeed, an excellent ministry from the pulpit should adorn every church that calls itself Anglican—for the preaching of the word is God's instrument for the salvation of human beings and the edification of the church.

For this reason, a quality theological education should be a high priority for Anglican churches everywhere, for the sake of the people of God. It is a matter of great sorrow that, in countries that can in fact afford to put ministerial candidates through an excellent process of training, church authorities are increasingly accepting for ordination people who have only studied at a meager level for a short period of time. It does not take a prophet to see that that policy will starve the churches of God of the food they need. Anglican churches that are experiencing the blessing of extraordinary spiritual and numerical growth will need support if they are to equip pastors for all those new believers. Such a theological education would equip pastors in their chief business, which is not management or counseling or community service, good though all these things are, but the knowledge of God in Scripture. They need a theological education deeply rooted in both Testaments of the Bible so that they can do their job—to preach Christ and him crucified.

And this says a great deal about the *model* of preaching that a church with these convictions should pursue. John Stott took his lead from the great expository preachers of the ancient church and the Reformation in the practice of preaching so that *Scripture itself might speak*. That practice can of course take many forms. But it has only one source. Preaching itself should be an act of submission to the text of Scripture, as preachers show themselves to be held in the grip of the word.

In every nation, pastors and congregations need to regain confidence in the power of God to work even through the trembling and lisping words of their preachers. By such words, God transforms lives. By such words are dictators challenged and outcasts called home. As Stott says:

> Through this written Word he continues to speak with a living voice powerfully. And the Church needs to listen attentively to his Word, since its health and maturity depend upon it. So pastors must expound it; it is to this they have been called. Whenever they do so with integrity, the voice of God is heard, and the Church is convicted and humbled, restored and reinvigorated, and transformed into an instrument for his use and glory.[56]

---

56. Stott, *I Believe in Preaching*, 133.

CHAPTER 4

The Gospel Signs: The Sacraments

The sacraments which Christ ordained preach God's word unto us, and therefore justify, and minister the Spirit to them that believe. . . . Dumb ceremonies are no sacraments, but superstitiousness. Christ's sacraments preach the faith of Christ, as his apostles did, and thereby justify. . . . And hereby mayest thou know the difference between Christ's signs or sacraments, and antichrist's signs or ceremonies; that Christ's signs speak, and antichrist's be dumb.

William Tyndale, *Obedience of a Christian Man*[1]

Anglican corporate worship is sacramental. This statement is almost a truism, so widely is it accepted. And yet the sacraments provide a source of internal division and disagreement within Anglicanism. As with other aspects of worship, the sixteenth-century Reformers were decisive in what they excluded but more vague in what they directed. The task of this chapter is, therefore, as complex

---

1. Quoted in Henry Walter, ed., *Doctrinal Treatises . . . by William Tyndale* (Cambridge: Parker Society, 1848), 283.

as its subject matter, if we are to understand what place the sacraments might have in a twenty-first-century version of Reformation Anglican worship. Nevertheless, we will be aided by the theology of worship I have already outlined in previous chapters in making sense of the role that the sacraments are to play in the common life of the church.

Augustine of Hippo's widely accepted definition of a sacrament is that it is "a visible form of an invisible grace."[2] This definition eventually made its way into the catechism of the Book of Common Prayer in 1604, where a sacrament was defined as "an outward and visible sign of an inward and spiritual grace, given unto us, ordained by Christ himself, as a means whereby we receive the same, and a pledge to assure us thereof."[3]

It is worth saying at the outset, however, that the term *sacrament* is not found in Scripture, nor is anything like that definition. This observation has no little significance: the idea that there is a class of ritual signs called *sacraments* postdates Scripture and is a development of the church's reflection on its own practices. A *sacramentum* was a pledge of allegiance made by a Roman soldier.[4] Its application to the symbolic actions of the Christian community was a recognition of their promissory nature: in them, the promises of God were declared and the promises of the believer announced. However, the invention of a category of such actions prompted the development of a theology that would support and articulate it. With such little scriptural support, much of what passes for sacramental theology reflects the church's speculations through the ages.

In the Middle Ages, the sacraments had become a highly developed system of ritualized acts. The Roman Catholic Church followed the great twelfth-century theologian Peter the Lombard, who fixed the number of sacraments at seven: baptism, the Lord's

---

2. This phrase is actually the summary by medieval theologian Peter the Lombard, *Sentences* 4.1.2, of Augustine's discussion in *Questions on the Heptateuch* 3.84.

3. F. E. Brightman, *The English Rite*, 2 vols. (London: Rivingtons, 1915), 1.clxxix–clxxxi, 2.787 (spelling modernized).

4. Charles Neil and J. M. Willoughby, *The Tutorial Prayerbook* (London: Harrison Trust, 1912), 288–90.

Supper, marriage, ordination, penance, confirmation, and extreme unction. Furthermore, these signs were held to work *ex opere operato* (Latin: "from the work of the thing worked")—which is to say, they had the power to automatically confer grace to the recipient. It was this claim in particular that the leading lights of the Continental Reformation would hotly dispute.

The Reformers and the Sacraments

There is no doubt that the evangelical Reformers of the sixteenth century saw themselves as making a deliberate move away from the view of the sacraments that had prevailed in the medieval church. They were in loud agreement that the sacramental system had become an avenue for the worst tendencies in medieval Christianity: emphasizing the priest, rather than Jesus, as mediator between God and his people; basing our relationship with God on what we must do for him rather than what Jesus has done for us on the cross; looking to an unbroken succession of human beings to convey the Holy Spirit, rather than God's own word; and so on. As they were, the sacraments were indicative of an entire theological system that needed to be dismantled and reconstituted from the ground up. And yet this proved elusive for the Reformers. They could not find agreement on a positive account of the sacraments, especially the Lord's Supper.

Most famously, Luther and Zwingli clashed at the Colloquy of Marburg in 1529, even though they had been called together by Philip I, Landgrave of Hesse, precisely for the purpose of presenting a united Protestant front. They engaged in four days of intense debate. Luther insisted that Jesus's phrase "This is my body" should be interpreted literally; consequently, he regarded Christ's human body as truly present in the Supper in a mystical fashion. Zwingli and Oecolampadius were equally determined that it should be understood figuratively, for they interpreted Jesus's words at the Last Supper in the light of John 6:63, "It is the Spirit who gives life; the flesh is no help at all." Hence, the only kind of life-giving eating of Christ in the Supper had to be spiritual, not carnal. Luther countered that if the flesh is no help at all, then the incarnation itself had no value. The fifteenth point of the colloquy recognized this sharp difference of opinion:

> Fifteenth, we all believe and hold concerning the Supper of our dear Lord Jesus Christ that both kinds should be used according to the institution by Christ; also that the Sacrament of the Altar is a sacrament of the true body and blood of Jesus Christ and that the spiritual partaking of the same body and blood is especially necessary for every Christian. Similarly, that the use of the sacrament, like the word, has been given and ordained by God Almighty in order that weak consciences may thereby be excited to faith by the Holy Spirit. And although at this time, we have not reached an agreement as to whether the true body and blood of Christ are bodily present in the bread and wine, nevertheless, each side should show Christian love to the other side insofar as conscience will permit, and both sides should diligently pray to Almighty God that through his Spirit he might confirm us in the right understanding. Amen.[5]

There was substantial and noteworthy agreement. The Reformers together rejected the understanding of the Mass as a substitutionary sacrifice in any way making a propitiation that belonged solely to the cross of Christ. They also agreed that both elements should be offered to the congregation (the practice of offering Communion "in one kind" was ubiquitous by the time of the Reformation). They were strongly agreed that taking the Lord's Supper was something an obedient Christian would do. But they were vociferous in their disagreement about what occurred *in* the rite itself. Luther asserted that Christ was present bodily at the Lord's Supper, whereas Zwingli did not. The other Reformers present at the Marburg Colloquy—among them Martin Bucer, who would go on to have a significant influence on the English Reformation in the 1540s and

---

5. Helmut T. Lehmann and Martin E. Lehmann, eds., *Luther's Works*, vol. 38, *Word and Sacrament IV* (Philadelphia: Fortress, 1971), 89.

1550s—leaned more toward Zwingli's position while still wanting to affirm a "spiritual presence."

The Church of England was somewhat of a latecomer to this discussion. Even following the break with Rome in the 1530s, Henry VIII did not permit a significant development of teaching on the sacraments. The Ten Articles (1536), though affirming a description of justification by faith, also held to the necessity of good works, baptism, and penance to a priest for salvation.[6] The Bishops' Book (1537), the popular name for *The Institution of a Christian Man*, incorporated the Ten Articles in its text but also added a description of the four other sacraments. On the Lord's Supper, it repeated the Ten Articles' statement that "under the form and figure of bread and wine, which we there presently do see and perceive by outward senses, is verily, substantially, and really contained and comprehended the very selfsame body and blood of our Saviour Jesus Christ."[7] This position was affirmed in the Six Articles (1539), in which the practice of withholding the cup from the laity was also defended.

Thus, the Henrician church never moved to a recognizably Protestant position on the sacraments, whether Lutheran or Reformed. The theological building blocks for a change were nonetheless beginning to be put into place; the doctrine of purgatory, to which the Mass was linked, was being attacked, and the doctrine of justification by faith alone did not allow for the same role in the salvation of a person's soul as the sacraments formerly had played in the Middle Ages. Furthermore, despite the official caution of the leading bishops, more radical views had certainly been circulating in England for at least two decades before Henry's death in 1547. William Tyndale's *Obedience of a Christian Man* (1528) had briefly expounded a view of the meaning and purpose of the sacraments

---

6. See, in particular, the description of the sacrament of penance, which included the statement about justification by faith, as well as the necessity of confession to a priest and good works for salvation. Charles Lloyd, *Formularies of Faith Put Forth by Authority during the Reign of Henry VIII* (Oxford: Oxford University Press, 1856), xx–xxv, 8–11.

7. Lloyd, *Formularies of Faith*, xxv, 11, 100.

that undermined later Anglican accounts; Tyndale argued that the sacraments were chiefly signs of God's promises, apprehended by faith as the accompanying word is preached.[8]

The Emergence of the Cranmerian View of the Sacraments

At an official level, a distinctively Anglican view of the sacraments would emerge only in the Edwardian era as Cranmer produced his new liturgies and issued the Forty-Two Articles. In keeping with other Reformed confessions, Cranmer reduced the number of sacraments from seven to two—namely, those instituted by Christ. Article 26, "Of the Sacraments,"[9] insisted that the sacraments are not to be venerated or carried about. Only those who worthily receive them realize the wholesome effect intended for them by Christ, "and yet not of the work wrought." That is to say, the view of the sacraments as having an automatic effect on anyone just by dint of having received them was expressly denied. Without faith, the sacraments are empty. Having said that, Cranmer also asserted that the sacraments are not simply badges signifying the profession of faith but are "effectual signs of grace" by which God does indeed act on believers.[10]

We shall have a chance to consider the significance of each of these moves shortly, but, as Oliver O'Donovan has pointed out, a "central theme" inspired all these revisions.[11] This could be found in the wording of Cranmer's Article 30,[12] which pointedly concludes the section of articles relating to the sacraments: "The Offering of Christ made once forever is the perfect redemption, the pacifying of God's displeasure and satisfaction for all the sins of the whole world, both original and actual: and there is none other satisfaction

---

8. William Tyndale and David Daniell, *The Obedience of a Christian Man*, Penguin Classics (New York: Penguin, 2000), 108–9.

9. Article 25 of the Thirty-Nine Articles, which were published in 1571.

10. Charles Hardwick, *A History of the Articles of Religion* (Cambridge: Deighton Bell, 1859), 306, 308.

11. Oliver O'Donovan, *On the Thirty Nine Articles: A Conversation with Tudor Christianity*, 2nd ed. (Exeter: Paternoster, 2011), 125.

12. Article 31 of the Thirty-Nine Articles.

for sin, but that alone."[13] This language was also a feature of the service of Holy Communion in the Book of Common Prayer:

> Almighty God our heavenly Father, which of thy tender mercy didst give thine only Son Jesus Christ, to suffer death upon the cross for our redemption, who made there (by his one oblation of himself once offered) a full, perfect, and sufficient sacrifice, oblation, and satisfaction for the sins of the whole world ... [14]

The single and sufficient atoning act in the entire history of humankind was that which Jesus himself accomplished on the cross. There was no further atonement needed. No further offering of any sacrifice could expunge the blot of sin. No other act could be described as meritorious. In fact, any thought that an additional act of atonement was being offered on the Table was an insult to the cross itself. Cranmer could not have been clearer on this subject—he wasn't reaching for vocabulary to express the inexpressible (as Archbishop Rowan Williams once suggested) but was underlining and even double-underlining the theological point: even as we lift the cup to our lips, we are to know that not this act but the act to which it points is the true act of sin-bearing atonement *without remainder*.[15] And this needed to be said not simply because of the way in which the sacramental system had functioned in the medieval period but also because of the universal human tendency to make idols out of signs. If there is majesty in Cranmer's language (and there certainly is), it is because he was seeking to clarify rather than obscure.

---

13. Hardwick, *History of the Articles*, 314.

14. Joseph Ketley, ed., *Two Liturgies ... of Edward VI* (Cambridge: Parker Society, 1844), 279.

15. In his sermon at St Mary the Virgin, Oxford, for the commemoration of the 450th anniversary of Cranmer's martyrdom, Williams said, "A liturgical language like Cranmer's hovers over meanings like a bird that never quite nests for good and all—or, to sharpen the image, like a bird of prey that never stoops for a kill." He later referenced the Prayer of Consecration specifically in this connection. In my respectful opinion, Williams could not be more in error: Cranmer is quite clear about what he is saying and what he is not saying. Rowan Williams, "The Martyrdom of Thomas Cranmer," Dr Rowan Williams (website), March 21, 2006, http://rowan williams.archbishopofcanterbury.org/articles.php/1599/the-martyrdom-of-thomas-cranmer -sermon-at-service-to-commemorate-the-450th-anniversary.

What then is the connection between the sacrament and the event for which it is a sign? Cranmer's final position on this issue had, of course, none of the metaphysical gymnastics that characterized medieval descriptions of the sacraments. His mature view, which he expressed in the founding formularies of the Church of England as a Protestant denomination under Edward VI, completely rejected the idea that the elements of the Communion service became the body and blood of Christ in substance, though with an unchanged appearance. Nor did he affirm Luther's variation on this, namely, that both the elements and Christ's body and blood were present. This Cranmer also explicitly denied. But there was still a sense in which the sacraments had for him a mediatory significance. Though Cranmer picked up the New Testament language of remembrance ("a perpetual memory") in describing the work the sacraments do, he was not content to leave it there, as Zwingli allegedly had done,[16] with bare recollection—a mental exercise on the part of the participant. Not at all: in the sacraments, by faith, Christ unites himself to us, so that we can be said truly to "feed on him in our hearts *by faith.*"

If the medieval doctrine had collapsed the sign into the thing it signified, the Zwinglian critique of that teaching had broken the link between the two. By the 1540s, the Continental theologians of the Reformed school had long been intent on mending the connection without slipping back into the past. Cranmer had Bucer, Bullinger, and Vermigli to advise him, and none of them were Zwinglian memorialists. What, then, was the Cranmerian proposal? Mark Chapman writes, "Cranmer's basic understanding of the sacrament was that spiritual presence was available by grace to those whom God had elected for salvation."[17] This "spiritual presence" was not an automatic or mechanical thing but a result of the prom-

16. Zwingli's real position was more complex than the caricature. See, for example, Bruce A. Ware, "The Meaning of the Lord's Supper in the Theology of Ulrich Zwingli (1484–1531)," in *The Lord's Supper: Remembering and Proclaiming Christ Until He Comes*, ed. Thomas R. Schreiner and Matthew R. Crawford (Nashville: B&H, 2010), 229–47.

17. Mark D. Chapman, *Anglican Theology* (London: T&T Clark, 2012), 36.

ise and the action of God in choosing to be present. And it was to be apprehended by faith, for the sacraments serve only as a judgment in the case of the unbeliever.

From his extensive research into the development of Cranmer's thinking as illustrated by the manuscripts from his massive eucharistic project in the 1530s and 1540s, Ashley Null shows how Cranmer was influenced by the Christology of Cyril of Alexandria in his developed theology of the Holy Communion.[18] From this newly rediscovered evidence, we can see that Cranmer believed that only the Spirit is present during the Lord's Supper, but the believer truly receives the full Christ, both in his humanity (i.e., body) and in his divinity (i.e., his spirit) because of Cranmer's understanding of the patristic principle (of Cyril and Chalcedon) that Christ always remains undivided.[19] In fact, in Cranmer's understanding, the Spirit by faith raises believers up to the heavenly place, where Christ's body is indeed present to be given to us.[20]

This view of the sacraments is not separate from or opposed to the Reformed theology of the spiritual word but an integral part of it. The word of God itself contains the promises declared in the sacraments and believed on by the faithful in the power of the Holy Spirit. Christ comes clothed in his word to the church; as authorized enactments of that evangelical word, the sacraments mediate the presence of Jesus Christ. If Christ is spiritually present to those

---

18. Ashley Null, "Cranmer's Reputation Reconsidered," in *Reformation Reputations,* ed. David Crankshaw and George Gross (London: Palgrave Macmillan, forthcoming).

19. In the text of a letter from the Basel Reformer Johannes Oecolampadius to Martin Bucer, dated September 3, 1530, a copy of which was in Cranmer's possession, we read (with Cranmer's underlining):

And although we may not say that [Christ's] salvific body is united with the bread or properly pressed between lips and teeth, we have never said, however, that because of this it can be separated from his divine spirit. On the contrary, we abhor that real separation as the worst plague. For Christ's body or humanity is not therefore divided from his deity, since the latter is immeasurable and everywhere, while the former is, however, circumscribed and occupying a fixed place. We say that his body and blood is nevertheless passed on and received together with the bread and the wine in a symbolic manner through faithful contemplation.

Cranmer annotated this passage with the words: "How the true body of Christ is present in the Supper."

20. Henry Jenkyns, ed., *The Remains of Thomas Cranmer,* 4 vols. (Oxford: Oxford University Press, 1833), 1:148.

gathered in faith as the word is read and preached, then he must also be present to them as they share in these evangelical signs. Even the formula for the Words of Administration from 1552—which represents the fullest extent of Cranmer's reform of the liturgy—clearly evokes a spiritual feeding "by faith, with thanksgiving": "Take and eat this, in remembrance that Christ died for thee, and feed on him in thy heart by faith, with thanksgiving."[21]

In debate with Bishop Stephen Gardiner over the Lord's Supper, Cranmer explained his own position thus:

> Although the sacramental tokens be only significations and fig-
> ures, yet doth Almighty God effectually work, in them that duly
> receive his sacraments, those divine and celestial operations
> which he hath promised, and by the sacraments be signified.
> For else they were vain and unfruitful sacraments, as well to the
> godly as to the ungodly. And therefore I never said of the whole
> Supper, that it is but a signification or a bare memory of Christ's
> death, but I teach that it is a spiritual refreshing, wherein our
> souls be fed and nourished with Christ's very flesh and blood
> to eternal life.[22]

This is a very carefully phrased statement. Note that Cranmer is clear that the elements of the Communion service are not more in substance than bread and wine. They are held to be "significations and figures" of the body and blood of Christ, his "very flesh and blood." Because God chooses to work effectually in these signs, the souls of the recipients are spiritually refreshed—not by chewing, in some literal sense, the very body and blood of Jesus but because the sign is, through faith, the means by which God works to attach us to the realities to which it points. As O'Donovan points out, for Cranmer, "the very nature of the sacrament is that in it Christ gives himself, really, to faith."[23] Later, Richard Hooker would echo this understanding: "The real presence of Christ's most blessed body

21. Ketley, *Two Liturgies*, 279.
22. Jenkyns, *Remains of Cranmer*, 3:229.
23. O'Donovan, *Thirty Nine Articles*, 128.

and blood is not therefore to be sought for in the sacrament, but in the worthy receiver of the sacrament."[24]

Baptism

As with so many things, on baptism the Reformers could agree more easily on what they denied than on what they would affirm. There were, of course, the so-called Anabaptists of the radical wing of the Reformation, who insisted on "believer's baptism" as against the practice of baptizing infants. By 1662 the liturgy contained a service for the baptism "of those who are of riper years" alongside the service for the baptism of infants, but with the expectation that infant baptism would be the norm. But what did the baptism of infants mean, and did it signal that they were regenerate? Does it work in some automatic sense, *ex opere operato*?

At the time of the New Testament, the Greek word *baptizō* had both a religious and a mundane sense. The word could simply indicate washing or immersing or soaking in water—something you might do to your hands, or to the cups and plates. But the ritual of water baptism had a long history in Judaism prior to the birth of Christianity. Ritual washings mentioned in the Old Testament code were acts of purification. Any reader of the New Testament would of course be aware of the proto-Christian baptismal ministry of John "the baptizer." John was not performing something unfamiliar to the Jews but carrying on a practice that had become common as a rite of entry into the community of God's people—one that signified repentance and purification. The relationship of this ritual to circumcision is unclear—why was it practiced when circumcision already existed as a rite of entry and a mark of membership?

But John's ministry was radical because he was suggesting that even Jews needed to "repent and be baptized." What's more, he foreshadowed one who would come after him and who would administer a baptism "with the Holy Spirit and fire" (Luke 3:16). Here

---

24. John Keble, ed., *The Works of . . . Richard Hooker*, 7th ed., 3 vols. (Oxford: Clarendon, 1888), 2:352 (*Laws of Ecclesiastical Polity*, 5.67.6).

something crucial is being said about Christian baptism: that it is an immersion not, in the first place, in water but in the Holy Spirit. The external washing of water baptism serves to point to the inner transformation of baptism in the fiery Spirit of God.

Jesus also makes a shocking metaphorical use of the idea of baptism in his words to James and John in Mark 10:38: "Are you able to drink the cup that I drink, or to be baptized with the baptism with which I am baptized?" The picture of baptism he is here evoking is something like drowning. His "baptism" is his atoning death. This strange, metaphorical use of the word to refer to Jesus's death is picked up by Paul in Romans 6:4: "We were buried therefore with him by baptism into death, in order that, just as Christ was raised from the dead by the glory of the Father, we too might walk in newness of life."

In Matthew's Gospel, Jesus's final words to his disciples are these:

> All authority in heaven and on earth has been given to me. Go therefore and make disciples of all nations, baptizing them in the name of the Father and of the Son and of the Holy Spirit, teaching them to observe all that I have commanded you. And behold, I am with you always, to the end of the age. (Matt. 28:18–20)

Did Jesus have in mind a water ceremony here? Which baptism was he talking about—the Holy Spirit baptism or an immersion of the body in water? At one level, the behavior of the early church told the story: in answer to this command, they immediately continued to symbolize the baptism of the Holy Spirit by the rite of water baptism. The direct result of the preaching of the gospel by Peter at Pentecost was that "those who received his word were baptized, and there were added that day about three thousand souls" (Acts 2:41). Peter had called them to "repent and be baptized." The Ethiopian eunuch asked to be baptized in water when Philip explained the gospel to him (Acts 8:36). Later, Peter encountered a group of Gentiles who had evidently experienced the baptism of the Holy Spirit, and he immediately exclaimed, "Can anyone withhold water for baptizing these people, who have received the Holy Spirit just as we have?" (Acts 10:47). This verse is particularly interesting because of the way in which the baptism by water *follows* the Spirit baptism. Water serves not as the instrument of the Spirit in a direct way but as a recognition of the Spirit's work.

While the Jewish ceremony of water baptism had been adapted as a way of speaking about the death of Christ, Christians would not do away with the ceremony of water baptism. It would become a symbol of baptism with the Holy Spirit. A later development, first expressed in the second century by Justin Martyr and others, was the idea that baptism with water was in fact the same thing as baptism in the Holy Spirit. The sign had become the thing that it symbolized. As we have just seen, the New Testament does not teach this at all. As Howe and Pascoe point out, "The typical pattern was that people came to faith and were *then* baptized in water as a public demonstration of their faith."[25]

But if faith precedes baptism in the New Testament, why then has the church practiced the baptism of infants since the earliest times? In a number of places in the book of Acts, Luke makes reference to the fact that a believer along with his or her household would be saved. Lydia (Acts 16:15), the Philippian jailer (Acts 16:31–33), and Crispus (Acts 18:8) were all baptized together with the members of their households. It is a reasonable inference that these included children along with the members of the other generations usually found living together in a Greco-Roman household. In its Jewish mode, baptism was customarily administered to children; so it would make sense if it was also administered to the children of Christian parents. Furthermore, the practice of circumcision, though not a complete parallel to that of baptism, was administered to baby boys (Gen. 17:9–14; Luke 2:21).

25. John W. Howe and Samuel C. Pascoe, *Our Anglican Heritage: Can an Ancient Church Be a Church of the Future?*, 2nd ed. (Eugene, OR: Cascade, 2010), loc. 1472 of 4959, Kindle.

There was no sense in which circumcision was held to work automatically—as if, by itself, the seal of circumcision was sufficient to make one a Jew. It was a symbol of a reality into which a person would grow, or else the symbol would be rendered empty. Likewise, what was declared by the inclusion of children in the sign of baptism was the inclusion of children in the promises and saving purposes of God in Jesus Christ. And, naturally, it meant that the child was to be brought up in the faith, just as Israelite children were to be. Of course, an Israelite child could grow up waywardly and in no sense accept the promise of which circumcision was a sign. Likewise, Christian baptism is not a guarantee that the child will be saved. Cranmer himself said that "in baptism those that come feignedly and those that come unfeignedly, both be washed with sacramental water, but both be not washed with the Holy Ghost."[26]

This leads us to a somewhat thorny issue in Anglican theology and history—the question of baptismal regeneration. There is no denying that the Baptismal Service has a form of wording that seems to state quite baldly that baptism works in an automatic sense. The minister declares, "Seeing now, dearly beloved brethren, that these children be regenerate..."[27] *Regeneration* is the term for new birth, which is that decisive change that the Holy Spirit works in a person to bring him or her conclusively into the kingdom of God. It is, in fact, Holy Spirit baptism.

In the nineteenth century, this phrase in the prayer book was the center of the famous "Gorham Case." In 1847, a country parson named George Gorham was recommended for the parish of Brampford Speke in Devon. The bishop of Exeter, Henry Phillpotts, examined Gorham and declared that his views on baptism were at odds with the doctrine of the Church of England. Gorham held the position that a child's baptism was a statement of regeneration conditional on acceptance of the promises later in life. Refused his

---

26. Jenkyns, *Remains of Cranmer*, 2:439.
27. Ketley, *Two Liturgies*, 289.

post by the bishop, Gorham took the matter through to the (secular) Privy Council and narrowly won.

The Articles are quite rightly against the idea that baptism works in an automatic way to regenerate the infant. Despite the stringent efforts of the Tractarians since the middle of the nineteenth century, it is impossible to read the prayer book as expressing unambiguously the view that by dint of the sacrament of baptism, the child receives regeneration, since it was not Cranmer's personal view,[28] nor was it the view expressed in the other formularies. Therefore, the intention of the author of the prayer book cannot have been to express the theology he elsewhere expressly repudiated.

How then should this declaration be read? We could simply acknowledge an inconsistency—a slip of the pen or an editorial lapse. But that seems unlikely. The best attempt to synthesize the statements of the prayer book and the formularies is that of Bishop J. C. Ryle in his book *Knots Untied*.[29] This question was fairly the knottiest of those knots. Ryle views the declaration of regeneration as "hypothetical," on the basis of a "charitable supposition." That is, the child is not automatically considered "regenerate," and may indeed turn out not to be; but he or she is presumed so until evidence to the contrary. Ryle points to other parts of the prayer book, including the funeral service, in which the same sense of a charitable supposition is accepted. Here also, then, the declaration that the child is regenerate is not, in fact, a denial that a worthy reception of the sacrament is essential. It is, however, a statement that such a worthy reception is to be prayed for and expected in the normal course of events. Baptism is, in this way, an anticipation of what God may do in a person's life.

When it is understood in the light of the central Reformation conviction about the gospel of free grace in Jesus Christ alone,

---

28. See Ashley Null, *Thomas Cranmer's Doctrine of Repentance: Renewing the Power to Love* (Oxford: Oxford University Press, 2000), 227–36.

29. Ryle wrote: "I cannot see that I ought to hold doctrines which make the Prayer-book clash and jar with the Articles and Homilies." John Charles Ryle, *Knots Untied*, 10th ed. (London: Thynne, 1898), 158.

which is received by faith, baptism is a most apt and edifying practice. It is rightly described as "effective" when a person, by faith, takes hold of the promises of God declared and demonstrated in baptism.

The Lord's Supper

In the church that the Reformers inherited, the service of the Mass was central and ubiquitous. As we have seen, the assertion of a new theology of justification also meant a revision of the place and meaning of the Lord's Supper in the life of the Christian. Grace is not somehow a property or a thing that can be conveyed in the elements of bread and wine themselves. Divine grace is an attitude of God—the attitude he demonstrates in the redemption of sinners on the cross of Jesus Christ. Grace, the Reformers argued, means that God is now disposed to forgive sinners and show them mercy. The sacraments, and especially the Lord's Supper, are then a sign of the grace of God revealed in the gospel. And, as such, like the preaching of the word, the Supper affects the very thing it points to. By speaking to the sinner of the grace of God, it enables the sinner by faith to enter into God's grace: to know it not simply objectively but subjectively. For Cranmer, grace is both God's attitude toward us and the Holy Spirit's work in us because of that attitude. The sacraments both convey the truth that God accepts us (i.e., his attitude) and are the effectual means for the Holy Spirit to strengthen our faith, binding us to God and, through that, renewing our affections—our love—for him over ourselves.

By translating the services of Holy Communion into English, Cranmer made a decisive statement about the nature of Christian faith. The meaning of the Eucharist was not hidden or mysterious or magical. It was to be declared and remembered. It was to be a species of the word—an intelligible sign of the gospel. Those who attended the Lord's Supper needed to know what they were eating; how else could they be moved to trust and love God in return?

The Lord's Supper was classified along with baptism as a practice commanded by Jesus himself, and so held a privileged place as one of the two sacraments on the reduced list of Reformation Anglicanism. The words that Jesus used at his Last Supper, "do this, as often as you drink it, in remembrance of me" (1 Cor. 11:25), indicate that he envisaged the disciples continuing to celebrate and remember his life-giving death. Paul's first letter to the Corinthians contains the lengthiest discussion of the practices of Christians as they gathered and, in particular, of "the Lord's Supper." The difficulty of course is that, as with almost everything else in the epistle, the discussion of the Lord's Supper takes place in response to abuses of the practice. We have no template or manual for its performance.

The particular context into which Paul speaks is the question about sharing in the pagan temple feasts. Can a Christian eat meat offered to idols? Paul replies:

> Therefore, my beloved, flee from idolatry. I speak as to sensible people; judge for yourselves what I say. The cup of blessing that we bless, is it not a participation in the blood of Christ? The bread that we break, is it not a participation in the body of Christ? Because there is one bread, we who are many are one body, for we all partake of the one bread. Consider the people of Israel: are not those who eat the sacrifices participants in the altar? What do I imply then? That food offered to idols is anything, or that an idol is anything? No, I imply that what pagans sacrifice they offer to demons and not to God. I do not want you to be participants with demons. You cannot drink the cup of the Lord and the cup of demons. You cannot partake of the table of the Lord and the table of demons. (1 Cor. 10:14–21)

As usual, Paul deploys a complex layering of symbol and metaphor. The "one bread" in which Christians share is Christ's body—a spiritual body, but one represented by the literal participation of Christians in eating the bread (and drinking the cup) that symbolizes that body. And that body is not only the broken body of Jesus of Nazareth but also the "body" of believers.

The problem Paul then addresses in the next chapter shows that the symbolism of the meal is deeply compromised by the way the Corinthians are going about it. The inequality and selfishness of the participants are unedifying. They destroy the very meaning of eating together in Christ, since the members do not eat together at all. Instead, says Paul, they should eat at home if they are hungry. The meal of the Lord is not for the indulgence of the physical appetites but for spiritual nourishment. The consequences of their selfishness are terrible, for eating and drinking in an unworthy manner is tantamount to a sin against the body and blood of the Lord himself (1 Cor. 11:27). The practice in the Christian church of having a purely token meal— a small piece of bread and a sip of wine, served in careful order—stems from taking good heed of the warnings here in 1 Corinthians 10–11.

Cranmer clearly made a careful study of these passages as he put the service of Holy Communion together. He wrote, "Christ ordained the sacrament to move and stir all men to friendship, love, and concord, and to put away all hatred, variance and discord, and to testify a brotherly and unfeigned love between all them that be the members of Christ."[30]

The rite of Holy Communion is a sign of the unity of the church in Christ, a sharing by all in the fellowship—the *koinōnia*—that comes with being bound into Christ. The oneness of the believers with each other is not achieved simply by eating together, but it is both an expression of that spiritual unity and a means by which it is encouraged. The moment of taking the sacrament involves a reflection on the fellowship of Christ's body—it calls for a "discernment of the body," as Paul puts it, such that those who eat and drink are not to do so as mere individuals. The Lord's Supper should not be thought to substitute for fellowship or to establish it on its own: to

---

30. Jenkyns, *Remains of Cranmer*, 2:297.

take the signs of the Communion and then not actually engage in the community of God's people perverts the very nature of the rite, just as a wedding after which the couple refused to speak to one another would be marriage in name only.

Paul warned the Corinthians very sternly about their abuse of the Lord's Supper:

> Whoever, therefore, eats the bread or drinks the cup of the Lord in an unworthy manner will be guilty concerning the body and blood of the Lord. Let a person examine himself, then, and so eat of the bread and drink of the cup. For anyone who eats and drinks without discerning the body eats and drinks judgment on himself. (1 Cor. 11:27–29)

In the 1549 service, Cranmer had ensured that no potential communicant would be in any doubt as to the seriousness of the rite and the spiritual consequences of partaking illegitimately. But this had the unfortunate consequence of turning people away from the service. The Supper had been intended for weekly participation, but, as MacCulloch speculates, "conscientious or shy potential communicants may have felt that they were not worthy to receive."[31] This led to the new emphasis on the services of Morning and Evening Prayer as the staple of the Church of England liturgy, with Holy Communion as a more occasional alternative. Only in the twentieth century was the Communion service returned to more frequent celebration—and, it is worth noting, contemporary revisions of the liturgy do not emphasize the Pauline warnings in the way that Cranmer did in 1549.

On the basis of Cranmer's theological understanding of the rite of Communion, then, it was indeed possible to partake of the elements and yet not validly receive the sacrament. Cranmer spoke of three ways in which the Supper may be eaten: "one spiritual only, another spiritual and sacramental both together, and the third

---

31. Diarmaid MacCulloch, *Thomas Cranmer: A Life* (New Haven, CT: Yale University Press, 1996), 510.

sacramental only."[32] As with baptism, it is important to grasp that a sacrament points to a spiritual reality. This means that it is perfectly possible to have the spiritual reality without partaking of the thing that points to it. One can easily "feed on Christ" without eating the Lord's Supper. It is also perfectly possible to consume the bread and the wine and yet not engage in spiritual eating at all, but, worse, engage in unspiritual eating. The unrepentant evildoers may come to the Lord's Table and eat; but it will not be effective for them, except as a judgment on them.

The form of eating in which the spiritual and the sacramental coincide is described by Cranmer thus: "There is another eating both spiritual and sacramental, when the visible sacrament is eaten with the mouth and Christ Himself is eaten with a true faith."[33] The sacrament of the Supper enacts a spiritual eating, which is the true form of faith. But by being itself a declaration of the gospel, it will also enable that spiritual eating of the faithful. It becomes in itself the instrument of God's blessing of his people in the sacrifice of Jesus Christ on the cross. For with each fresh declaration of the gospel, God sends forth his Holy Spirit anew. In this way, the sacrament can be understood as an "effectual sign of grace."

As we have seen, the English Reformers were insistent that the Lord's Supper was not in any way a repetition of Christ's once-for-all sacrifice. In support of this theology, they pursued a number of alterations in the practice of the rite. Chief among these was the attempt to substitute tables for altars in English churches, both physically and in terminology. The word *altar* signified the making of a sacrifice; a table was, rather, the place where people might gather to eat with one another. Paul himself makes that distinction

---

32. Jenkyns, *Remains of Cranmer*, 3:319. He also wrote:

I teach that no man can eat Christ's flesh and drink His blood but spiritually, which, forasmuch as evil men do not, although they eat the sacramental bread until their bellies be full, and drink the wine until they be drunken, yet eat they neither Christ's flesh, nor drink his blood, neither in the sacrament nor without the sacrament, because they cannot be eaten and drunken but by spirit and faith, whereof ungodly men be destitute, being nothing but world and flesh. (3:316)

33. Jenkyns, *Remains of Cranmer*, 3:319.

in 1 Corinthians 10, where he contrasts the "table" of the Lord's Supper with the "altar" of pagan sacrifices. In keeping with this, the 1552 Book of Common Prayer commanded that "the Table having at the Communion time a fair white linen cloth upon it, shall stand in the body of the Church, or in the chancel, where Morning prayer and Evening prayer be appointed to be said."[34] The table was to be made of wood and not fixed into position but moveable. The reintroduction of stone altars did not occur until well into the nineteenth century, under the influence of the Oxford movement; it signaled a return (in the minds of some) to a pre-Reformation theology of the Lord's Supper.

The elements of the Communion service were not in any sense to become the objects of veneration. As Cranmer's Article 29[35] states: "The Sacrament of the Lord's Supper was not commanded to be kept, carried about, lifted up, nor worshiped."[36] The elements were not to be elevated by the minister in the Communion service; and the priest could take any leftover consecrated bread and wine for his domestic use, which indicated that it was not inherently transformed in some way. The language of "consecration" was still used but did not indicate a change in the essence of the things. Rather, it indicated that the ordinary stuff of bread and wine, grain and grape, was being put to holy use.

All of these symbolic alterations to the practice of Communion were a result of the Reformers' abhorrence (and that's not too strong a way to put it) of the doctrine of transubstantiation—in which the bread and wine were held actually to become the body and blood of Christ and thence to be consumed by the communicants.[37] We should remember that it was on account of their

---

34. Ketley, *Two Liturgies*, 265.
35. Article 28 of the Thirty-Nine Articles.
36. Hardwick, *History of the Articles*, 314.
37. A note about terminology is certainly in order. The doctrine of transubstantiation is an explanation of how Christ is really present in the elements at the Lord's Supper. That is, it is the mechanism by which the "real presence" is said to be effected in the bread and the wine, such that Christ is *in* them. The elements are held to be actually transformed, even though, to the senses, the blood and body are still experienced as bread and wine.

testimony against this specific teaching that the leading Reformers were martyred in the reign of Queen Mary (1553–1558). The publication of *De corpora et sanguine Domini* (*On the Body and Blood of the Lord*) in 1531, by the medieval monk Ratramnus (d. 870), was seized upon by evangelical scholars as a demonstration that the theology of transubstantiation was a later development and not the unanimous testimony of the historic church. Ratramnus had argued that the bread and the wine did not truly become the body and blood of Christ but figuratively represented them. Nicholas Ridley, and later, after an exhaustive study of the fathers, Cranmer himself, became convinced that Ratramnus was correct in denying the bodily presence of Christ at the Eucharist. In the 1552 book we find that there is no sense in which a presence of Christ is "localized" (i.e., located) within the elements on the table.

Why did this matter? It mattered because the Reformers felt that a doctrine of the real presence in the Eucharist undermined the heart of the gospel of justification by faith and the unique once-for-all work of Jesus Christ on the cross. First, insisting on some kind of change in the elements detracted from the real purpose of the Supper, which was to make a change in the hearts of the faithful recipients, supernaturally drawing their wills afresh from self-centeredness to loving God and their neighbors more. Second, a presence located in the bread and wine suggested that Christ's body was being offered now, upon the Table, as a fresh offering, crucifying the Lord all over again. As Cranmer wrote,

> If they make every day the same oblation and sacrifice for sin that Christ himself made, and the oblation that he made was his death and the effusion of his most precious blood upon the cross for our redemption and price of our sins; then followeth it of necessity, that they every day slay Christ and shed his blood.[38]

---

38. Jenkyns, *Remains of Cranmer*, 2:453.

And yet, the creeds declared that the Lord had taken on a resurrected body and now reigns on high, from whence "he shall come to judge both the quick and the dead: Whose kingdom shall have no end."[39]

In denying a localized presence of Christ in the bread and the wine, however, the leaders of the English Reformation did not want to say that Christ was not present at all. He was not present in some way in the elements; but he was present to the communicant spiritually, by faith. Or, perhaps more accurately, the believer was by faith made present in Christ in the heavenly realms in the eating of the Supper—drawn into the heavenly throne room. That was the meaning of the *Sursum Corda*, the moment in the service when the congregation is called to "lift up your hearts!" and the people respond, "We lift them to the Lord!" They are being brought into the presence of the heavenly Lord, rather than the other way around.

Cranmer made both points about the presence in the brief he presented at his disputation on the Lord's Supper while being held prisoner under Mary at Oxford on April 16, 1555:

> When [Christ] said, *'Eat ye; this is my body'* . . . [he meant] that bread which by nature is usual and common with us, which is taken of the fruit of the ground, compacted by the uniting of many grains together, made by man . . . of this same bread, I say, and of any uncertain and wandering substance, the old fathers say that Christ spake these words, *'Eat ye; this is my body'*. . . . And so the doctors do call this speaking of Christ tropical, figurative, anagogical, allegorical; which they do interpret after this sort, that although the substance of bread and wine do remain, and be received of the faithful, yet notwithstanding, Christ changed the appellation thereof, and called the bread by the name of his flesh . . . ; not that it is so in very deed, but signified in a mystery: so that we should consider, not what they be in their own nature, but what they import to us and signify; and should

---

39. Quoted in the Book of Common Prayer, 1662.

understand the sacrament, not carnally, but spiritually; and should attend, not to the visible nature of the sacraments . . . ; but that, lifting up our minds, we should look up to the blood of Christ with our faith, should touch him with our mind, and receive him with our inward man; and that, being like eagles in this life, we should fly up into heaven in our hearts, where that Lamb is resident at the right hand of his Father . . . ; being made the guests of Christ, having him dwelling in us through the grace of his true nature, and through the virtue and efficacy of his whole passion; being no less assured and certified that we are fed spiritually unto eternal life by Christ's flesh crucified, and by his blood shed, the true food of our minds, than that our bodies be fed with meat and drink in this life.[40]

Cranmer was happy to label the wine in the cup "blood" and the bread on the table "body," since this is what Christ did. But Christ did so not because the elements had *become* his body and blood but because the elements were *symbols* of those things. Yet, by the gospel word there proclaimed, God chooses to work by the Holy Spirit in the sacrament. Therefore, the bread and the wine may rightly be called the "body" and "blood," since the Holy Spirit uses these symbols to quicken the faith of believers to ascend to heaven where the physical body of Christ is, so that the faithful can experience ever-closer union with him and give him true worship there.

Who should celebrate at the Lord's Table? For the Reformers of the Church of England, there was no question that it should be the chief elder of the congregation, the ordained priest. But the notion of priesthood did not, in their consideration of the matter, imply a sacerdotal ministry, in which an ordained officer acted as the priests in the Old Testament cult had done and made sacrifices on behalf of the people to atone for sin. The book of Hebrews was brought forward as testimony that the old

---

40. Jenkyns, *Remains of Cranmer*, 4:16–18.

covenant notion of priesthood had been consummated in the definitive atonement offered by Christ on the cross. Likewise, it could easily be pointed out from the Pastoral Epistles that the Christian ministry as envisaged by Paul was not at all sacerdotal in nature. The church as a whole was to inherit the title of "royal priesthood" (1 Pet. 2:9), certainly. But this was an indication of their role in declaring the praises of God to the world—it was part of the task of mission.

The New Testament does use the language of sacrifice to speak of the response of believers, in Romans 12:1–2 and in Hebrews 13; but the sacrifice thereby encouraged is not an atoning sacrifice but, rather, a sacrifice of thanksgiving and praise in response to the atonement for sin made available in Christ. Nevertheless, the principle of orderly worship meant that the ordained ministers were held responsible for almost every activity in the church service. In that respect, not much had changed since before the Reformation. This was not intended to affirm them as sacerdotal ministers in the manner of the Roman Catholic priesthood; rather, they were the responsible elders of the congregation.

As with every aspect of Reformation Anglican worship, the theology of the Holy Communion as expressed in the Book of Common Prayer and in the thought of its leading proponents is designed to reflect the gospel of justification by grace through faith alone. It casts the believers as the recipients of grace who respond with gratitude. However, this sacramental theology did not maintain its hold on much of Anglicanism in the following decades. Without always simply reinstituting a Roman doctrine of transubstantiation, Anglican theologians frequently went back to a view more in keeping with the real presence theology, and they held a view of the priesthood consistent with that conviction. This is a good place to recall one of the aims of this book: my conviction is not that the Reformation Anglican position is more authentically Anglican than the alternatives, but that it is biblically and theologically more convincing, and more consistent with the essence of the Christian gospel.

The Sacraments in the Contemporary Global Anglican Church

As I have already noted, the Oxford movement of the nineteenth century had a profound impact on the theology and practice of the sacraments in local Anglican congregations worldwide. The practices of elevating the host and reserving the sacrament, the replacing of wooden tables with stone altars, and the adoption of more elaborate priestly vestments represented the normalization of a theology of the Eucharist and of the priesthood decidedly at odds with that of the Reformation era. In many places, a theology of the real presence at the Eucharist and baptismal regeneration has become *the* Anglican theology. This does not necessarily represent a return to medieval Catholicism per se; but revised liturgies have made Catholic interpretations of the Eucharist more explicit.

At the same time, the greater participation of lay people in the gathering of God's church has become customary since the 1960s: from lay preaching to leading prayers and reading Scripture. The only worship activity reserved for ordained clergy exclusively is that of administering the Lord's Supper. This is an unforeseen imbalance, further isolating this single activity from the others. The synod in my own diocese, the diocese of Sydney, Australia, has long advocated allowing lay administration at the Lord's Supper so as to make clear the non-sacerdotal nature of the office of priest (or presbyter, to use the alternative nomenclature preferred in Sydney) and to maintain the theological principles of the Reformation in a new context. This proposal has not gained much traction across the Anglican Communion, but neither has it met with much serious theological engagement on the biblical terms on which it is proposed.

Nevertheless, the thought that contemporary Anglicans might need to downplay the sacraments to avert a serious overemphasis on them is pitiable. The correct antidote to a mistaken teaching is true teaching. The gospel signs retain their power to nourish believers in their faith and to assure them of the work of God in their lives. The practice of the sacraments reminds the faithful that God is not simply distant and transcendent but also present and active among them.

CHAPTER 5

Prayers of Grace

There is nothing in all man's life, well beloved in our
Saviour Christ, so needful to be spoken of, and daily to
be called upon, as hearty, zealous, and devout prayer;
the necessity whereof is so great, that without it nothing
may be well obtained at God's hand.

"An Homily or Sermon Concerning Prayer," second Book of
Homilies[1]

God's breath in man returning to his birth.

George Herbert, "Prayer," in *The Temple*[2]

Prayer, it is not too bold to say, is a human universal. Human beings
at all times and in all places (if not every individual) have called out
to the divine Being or beings—whether for help or protection, or to
praise or give thanks, or to call down curses on an enemy's head.
At one level, this makes prayer not so very interesting, since it is

1. Quoted in John Griffiths, *Two Books of Homilies* (Oxford: Oxford University Press, 1859), 320.
2. Quoted in A. B. Grosart, ed., *The Poetical Works of George Herbert* (London: George Bell, 1886), 72.

ubiquitous. The similarities between the forms of prayer are far less significant than the differences. Christian prayer claims not simply to be another form of prayer but to be indicative of a specifically defined relationship to the divine being, whom we call on as "Father." As we have seen already, the Christian approaches God only on the basis of God's prior approach. Thus, like the other aspects of Christian worship, prayer is fundamentally a response to who God reveals himself to be.

The theological transformation heralded at the Reformation was, as we have also seen, a transformation of Christian piety in all its forms. This was no less evident in the matter of prayer than anywhere else. Though perhaps prayer as a subject attracted less controversy than other aspects of Christian corporate worship, still a very significant reconstitution of the nature and meaning of prayer was being undertaken. It doesn't take much reflection to understand why this was so. What prayer is in essence is very much determined by the object of prayer. If, with Luther, the evangelicals of the Reformation discovered afresh the grace and mercy of God in combination with (and not in tension with) his righteousness, then it makes sense to expect from them a new understanding of what prayer is and what prayer does.

The English Reformers, like their European counterparts, were keen to provide, in their freshly minted orders of service, a school for prayer in the vernacular tongue. At first, this new kind of worship was very confusing to the laity. As one member told her neighbor, "Alas, gossip, what shall we now do at church, since all the saints are taken away, since all the goodly sights we were wont to have are gone, since we cannot hear the like piping, singing, chanting, and playing upon the organs, that we could before?"[3] Indeed, this confusion included even the most basic understanding of how one prayed during the service. Since the medieval liturgy was in Latin and, thus, not understood by the people, the laity focused on

---

3. Griffiths, *Two Books of Homilies*, 349.

their own private devotions rather than what the priest was saying. However, "An Homily on the Right Use of the Church" pointed out that with the arrival of a vernacular liturgy, traditional private acts of piety during worship were contrary to Scripture: "St. Paul teacheth . . . *Glorifying God with one spirit and mouth*, which cannot be when every man and woman, in [separate] pretence of devotion, prayeth privately, one asking, another giving thanks, another reading doctrine, and forceth not to hear the common prayer of the minister."[4] Consequently, "On Common Prayer and Sacraments" found it necessary to teach the people how to worship as good Protestants:

> Whiles our minister is in rehearsing the prayer that is made in the name of us all, we must give diligent ear to the words spoken by him, and in heart beg at God's hand those things that he beggeth in words. And, to signify that we so do, we say, Amen, at the end of the prayer that he maketh in the name of us all.[5]

Hence, the Book of Common Prayer was a repository not only of congregational prayers but also of prayers that could be learned and repeated by any congregation member. The Reformers took great care, as we shall see, to reflect in their composition of prayers for the people the theology of divine grace mediated only in Christ—and the proper human response—that they had so lately learned. They were responding to the division of labor so characteristic of the medieval church, in which the monasteries provided a specialized—and amply funded—service of praying. Prayer became the privileged task of every believer.

In this chapter I shall seek to outline, from the three homilies on prayer that appeared in 1563, a Reformation Anglican approach to prayer. We shall note that prayer was not simply those prayers authorized for use in common worship. The Reformers were adamant that prayer was a basic property of the Christian life for every

---

4. Griffiths, *Two Books of Homilies*, 162–63.
5. Griffiths, *Two Books of Homilies*, 358.

believer. Next, by means of an examination of some of the prayers in the Book of Common Prayer itself, we shall see how Cranmer and others put into practice their convictions about prayer in the light of the theology of grace.

Prayer in Medieval Christianity

In medieval Christianity, there had developed a veritable industry of prayer. We have already seen how, in the chantry houses of Europe, the monastic movement made the business of prayer its very own. The demands of praying several times a day were too onerous for the average Christian. The monks, friars, nuns, and other religious functionaries took the burden on themselves on behalf of the rest of the social order. As a result, they lived apart, sequestered from the everyday concerns of family life, political life, and economic life.

What was this prayer for? Those who prayed had a job to do to plead with God on behalf of society for its protection and its well-being. They prayed against the uncertainties of human life—against plague and pestilence, famine and misfortune. They not only prayed to God but also sought the help of the host of saints, and of the Virgin Mary. Luther himself spoke of calling out to St. Anne in the midst of a mighty storm in which he was caught sometime in his youth.[6]

An ordinary Christian's spiritual life was not expected to involve prayer in the sense that we have become familiar with since the Reformation era. Church services were not in the vernacular, and so, as we have seen, the laity could not actively or knowingly participate in the prayers of the service. However, there was, even prior to the Reformation, a widespread dissatisfaction with this prayerlessness among the laity, and a number of lay spiritual movements sprang up reflecting this hunger for something more spiritually authentic.

---

6. Roland H. Bainton, *Here I Stand: A Life of Martin Luther* (Peabody, MA: Hendrickson, 2009), 11–16.

The *Devotio Moderna* was one of these, arising in the Netherlands at the end of the fourteenth century. Dissatisfied with the state of the church and the absence of piety among the clergy, Dutch scholar Geert Groote preached for a return to a simple and pious way of life saturated with meditation and prayer. The communities of lay people that took root as a result of his teachings became known as the Brethren of the Common Life. These communities consisted mainly of laymen who did not take vows.

They did, however, devote themselves to Scripture and prayer and to looking after the poor. Their influence should not be underestimated, since Erasmus and Luther both had degrees of contact with their teachings; and perhaps the most influential work of medieval piety, Thomas à Kempis's *Imitation of Christ*, composed in the fifteenth century, was a product of this new turn in piety.

The piety of *The Imitation of Christ* links an intense inwardness to a life of quiet and humble good works—as far removed from the world as possible. Thomas emphasizes silence and solitude as the necessary contexts for the life modeled after Christ. The life of intense meditation is the pathway to the heavenly throne, and the study of the life of Christ is necessary so as to inculcate those virtues that the Christian requires. Thomas writes, "Grace is always given to him who is duly grateful, and what is [usually] to be given to the humble will be taken away from the proud."[7] Note here that gratefulness is the trigger for the divine gift of grace, and not simply a response to it. Prayer is a movement of the individual soul toward God in devotion.

Thus, even while there was a surge in lay piety in the latter Middle Ages, it modeled itself on the piety of monasticism. Prayer in the *Devotio Moderna* was still a matter of seeking to meet God on terms that pleased him, of impressing upon God the humility and the devotion of the individual soul. There was, as Roman Catholic theologian Hans Urs von Balthasar was later to point out,

---

7. Thomas à Kempis, *The Imitation of Christ* (Peabody, MA: Hendrickson, 2004), 46.

no cross in this Christianity: "There is no mention of the mediation of the God-man, of access through Christ, in the Holy Spirit, to the Father."[8] Jesus is to be imitated but, strangely, imitated by a withdrawal from the world that he himself never modeled. And prayer is made possible not through or on account of his work but almost in denial of it.

Prayer in the Homilies

The theology of prayer that we encounter in the series of sermons on prayer from the second Book of Homilies (1563), probably penned by Bishop John Jewel of Salisbury,[9] is of an entirely different order. It is no less zealous for the Christian practice of regular, disciplined prayer. But prayer serves an altogether different purpose in the Christian life, since it does not in and of itself draw the believer closer to God.[10]

The first homily on prayer, "An Homily or Sermon concerning Prayer," falls into three parts.[11] In the first of these, Jewel points out that though God knows our needs even before we ask him, prayer is still a great benefit to us. Our prayers do not surprise God, but they are God's ordained means for strengthening our faith in him: "There is nothing more expedient or needful for mankind in all the world than prayer."[12] The purpose of prayer is that we might indeed learn thankfulness.

> To the intent we might acknowledge him to be the Giver of all good things, and behave ourselves thankfully towards him in that behalf, loving, fearing, and worshiping him sincerely and truly, as we ought to do, he hath profitably and wisely ordained that in time of necessity we should humble ourselves in his

---

8. Hans Urs von Balthasar, *The Glory of the Lord*, vol. 5, *The Realm of Metaphysics in the Modern Age* (Cambridge: Cambridge University Press, 2001), 103–4.

9. Griffiths, *Two Books of Homilies*, xxxiii.

10. For the following analysis on prayer in the homilies, see Gerald Bray, "Prayer in the English Reformation: Part 1," *Credo* 4, no. 4 (2014): 24–31, and "Prayer in the English Reformation: Part 2," *Credo* 4, no. 4 (2014): 32–41.

11. Griffiths, *Two Books of Homilies*, 320–38.

12. Griffiths, *Two Books of Homilies*, 321.

sight, pour out the secrets of our heart before him, and crave help at his hands, with continual, earnest, and devout prayer.[13]

In the second part of the homily, the emphasis turns to the God to whom the Christian prays. It would be useless to turn to God in our moment of need if God were unable to help us. But he is certainly able. And furthermore, he is willing to help, is able to hear our prayers, and—even better—knows what we need better than we do. These divine qualities make him the sole worthy recipient of our prayers. Indeed, it is faith that directs our prayers, and if our faith is in any other than the God who is powerful, knowledgeable, and generous, then we blaspheme him. If prayer is, as Augustine says, a lifting up of the mind to God—more an inward disposition of the heart than a form of words on the lips—then we have no business, and no comfort in, praying to someone who cannot truly know our minds or our hearts.

The critique of the medieval system of prayers to the saints is scarcely veiled here. But this is not simply a polemical point. It is a corollary of the Reformation theology of justification by faith in Christ alone: "Christ is our only mediator and intercessor with God and . . . we must seek and run to no other." In Christ we perceive that God is not dangerous or unpredictable, judge of all though he is. He is, rather, merciful and just, and "[near] unto them that call upon him in faith and truth."[14] We observe in Jesus Christ God's compassionate love and his call to seek him. A person's sins are not an obstacle to prayer—not because God overlooks these sins but because, in Christ, atonement is made for them. Taking up the Christology of the epistle to the Hebrews, the homily emphasizes Christ's ongoing role as our mediator through his everlasting priesthood. Our access to the Father, to whom we pray, is sufficiently and completely obtained by Jesus Christ. And this is the ground for the Christian confidence that we are heard when we pray: not that we

---

13. Griffiths, *Two Books of Homilies*, 320.
14. Griffiths, *Two Books of Homilies*, 327.

are sufficiently abject or have found the right formula of words or have finally thanked him enough. Everything needed has been done for us.

For what ought the Christian to pray? The third part of the homily urges the Christian to pray to God wisely, remembering that we pray to the "heavenly King, who is only delighted with justice and equity."[15] The Christian should pray for his or her own spiritual and physical well-being. The needs of the soul should be given higher priority than those of the body as we remember which have greater importance. However, seeking the honor and glory of God, and not our own, is the key to making our petitions. Love (as Gerald Bray notes)[16] is the key: "Whomsoever we are bound by express commandment to love, for those also we are bound in conscience to pray."[17] Prayer expresses love; and the love of God knows no bounds. Therefore, prayers should be offered for kings and rulers, for ministers, for fellow Christians, and for those not Christian—indeed for all people on the earth.

Just as the Christian is not to pray to the saints, so he or she is not to pray for the dead. There is no commandment in the Bible to do so; and furthermore, the homily argues (in keeping with Reformation orthodoxy on this matter) that the judgment of God is final after death. Purgatory is held to be a fiction, and a disastrous one at that, since it undermines the cross of Christ as the only sure mediation between God and human beings. And the idea that our prayers could in some sense speed the soul's passage through purgatory is disastrous, since (once again) it implies that the cross is insufficient for the purpose. The cross of Christ is "that purgatory wherein all Christian men must put their whole trust and confidence, nothing doubting but, if they truly repent them of their sins, and die in perfect faith, that then they shall forthwith pass from death to life."[18]

---

15. Griffiths, *Two Books of Homilies*, 332.

16. "Prayer is primarily an expression of love—our love for God and the love that he has commanded us to have for our fellow men." Bray, "Prayer in the English Reformation: Part 1," 29.

17. Griffiths, *Two Books of Homilies*, 335.

18. Griffiths, *Two Books of Homilies*, 337–38.

If that were not enough, no prayers of human beings could release a soul from purgatory.

The first of these homilies on prayer makes no distinction between the private prayer of the individual Christian and public prayers of the gathered community of faith. The second in the series, "An Homily of the Place and Time of Prayer," is concerned with more obviously practical matters.[19] The homilist commends the practice of keeping the Christian Sabbath, Sunday, for meeting together with God's people, and addresses our common prayers to God. Distractions of work and recreation ought to be put aside by the community on these occasions. Furthermore, there ought to be places constructed for prayer, so that people can gather there to do so. The true temples of God are in fact the bodies and minds of his people: there is no suggestion that a church building substitutes for this in any way. And yet, there is a good purpose in building meeting places for the people of God that encourage them in their reverent seeking after God. Likewise, there is no place or time that is not fit for prayer. But setting aside a particular time and place for prayer is an edifying practice to be greatly encouraged.

The third homily is entitled "An Homily Wherein Is Declared That Common Prayer and Sacraments Ought to Be Ministered in a Tongue That Is Understanded of the Hearers."[20] The title promises an exposition of a characteristic Reformation theme: that common worship ought to take place audibly and in the vernacular, not in Latin. But there is a great deal more in this somewhat lengthier sermon than the title suggests. The homilist takes up a definition of prayer that Augustine was thought to have authored: "Prayer is that devotion of the mind, that is to say, the returning to God through a godly and humble affection; which affection is a certain willing, and sweet inclining of the mind itself towards God."[21]

---

19. Griffiths, *Two Books of Homilies*, 339–51.
20. Griffiths, *Two Books of Homilies*, 352–67.
21. Griffiths, *Two Books of Homilies*, 352 (spelling modernized).

There are, for the homilist, three kinds of prayer—two being private and a third "common." The first is silent prayer that lifts up the mind to God, as exemplified by Hannah, the mother of Samuel in 1 Samuel 1. This is the sort of prayer that all Christians should be praying continually. The second kind is the private prayer that Jesus describes in Matthew 6, whereby the voice is used, but in private without great display of piety, since insincere posturing is so great a temptation for human beings. But there is also a place for public or common prayer, since Scripture contains so many instances of it. And, thus, for the preacher of this homily, there is no excuse for negligence in common prayer. In common prayer the people of God are united to call on him, which in itself is a demonstration of his power.

The practice of common prayer should, though, follow the principles for corporate worship already outlined in the writings of Cranmer and the other Reformers. That is, "Let all things be done to edifying" (1 Cor. 14:26). Public prayers are not edifying if offered in a language that people simply do not understand. They cannot be edified if those praying do not comprehend what they are praying. This is as much a reason to forbid Latin as it is to be reticent about the public exercise of speaking in tongues without interpretation. It is also a reason to commend careful instruction of the people in what they are praying so that their "Amen" is an informed assent. Babbling a formula of words is of no spiritual value at all, and indeed is condemned most roundly in Scripture. If prayer is "that devotion of the mind which enforceth the heart to lift up itself to God," then the person who prays aloud without understanding what he or she is praying cannot be said to be praying at all.[22] Congregants should be given a chance to prepare their hearts to pray, so that they are not simply mouthing what is said without a readiness to agree sincerely.

As we have seen, the homilies are not offering a culturally distinctive preference for a new style of praying but are applying

---

22. Griffiths, *Two Books of Homilies*, 364.

the theology of the Reformation to the Christian life as consistently and biblically as possible. To pray together is a significant reason Christians gather. But they gather to pray to the God who has drawn them to himself in Christ, justifying them freely by his grace. They pray to God with no need for any other mediator than Christ himself, and as sinners who are nonetheless confident in Christ of meeting a gracious and merciful God in their hour of need.

And they are to pray in intelligible words—words they understand. The prayer of the Christian as a creature of the word of God corresponds to that word by being something understood. There is no hint that prayer is a kind of mindless repetition of a formula of talismanic sounds. Though there is a place for the inarticulate groanings of the inner being in private prayer, this is not tantamount to a form of mystical prayer. Public prayer must edify the congregation; congregants can only truly say "Amen," and thus only truly pray, if they hear and understand what is prayed.

Prayer in the Book of Common Prayer

What then of prayer in the Book of Common Prayer? It is notable enough that it is called a *prayer* book and not by some other title— giving a hint as to what Cranmer and others thought they were doing by preparing their liturgies. One feature that is prominent from the 1549 book onward is the services for Morning and Evening Prayer designed as a replacement for the seven "offices of prayer" that framed the monastic life. Stemming from Basil's provision for those who had secular jobs,[23] these offices were intended to be daily services of prayer accessible to any in the community who should be able to gather—a sign that, at least in principle, the routine of daily prayer was not the particular responsibility of a professionalized group but belonged to the laity as well.

---

23. See Cranmer's annotation in his copy of D. Erasmus, ed., *En amice lector thesaurum damus D. Basilium sua lingua loquentem* (Basel: H. Froben, 1532), 18, now held in the John Rylands Library, Manchester University, catalog no. 18173.

The Book of Common Prayer was intended to be a school for prayer. Its prayers were crafted to be vivid in imagery and easily memorable. Take, for example, the line "we have erred and strayed from thy ways, like lost sheep," from the General Confession (added in 1552).[24] The biblical and agricultural image is vivid; it conveys exactly what is intended, with the language of Isaiah 53 in the not-too-distant background. The rhythm of the line (technically speaking "anapestic") draws emphasis on the key words "strayed," "ways," and "sheep." The language is concrete and direct. At its best, the Book of Common Prayer in its various editions achieved this didactic effect very well indeed.

Furthermore, public prayer was designed to be truly congregational. It was certainly to be led by the minister, but the congregation was invited to pray aloud, either alongside him or in response. The place of the choir was, in effect, taken by the congregation, whose members were now to find their voices. Whether this is what happened in practice is doubtful. No doubt illiteracy and inattentiveness meant that the minister would continue to read the service for the most part on his own. Nevertheless, there was in this form of service an intention to encourage participation by the congregation as a reflection of Cranmer's more egalitarian theology.

We should not be slow to notice how Scripture informs the prayers that are embedded in the services of the Book of Common Prayer. Not only are various phrases, sentences, and images taken from Scripture, but lengthy parts of Scripture are included in full. The Lord's Prayer, the *Nunc Dimittis*, the *Magnificat*, and Psalms 95, 98, and 67 are given prominence. In addition, the Psalms are to be said or sung. Scriptural language is not used exclusively, but these particular passages of Scripture are made to serve as the prayers that the people should pray. This feature of the new liturgy reminds us that Scripture itself is a kind of prayer book—not simply

24. Joseph Ketley, ed., *Two Liturgies . . . of Edward VI* (Cambridge: Parker Society, 1844), 218.

to be read as God's word to us but also to serve, as the occasion warrants, as our word to God.

How is God to be addressed? How does the Reformation Anglican liturgy script calling on God for the people of God? The General Confession of the Communion service is an example: "Almighty God, Father of our Lord Jesus Christ, Maker of all things, Judge of all men."[25] We should add just one further repeated theme: he is also the "merciful Father."[26] The God of the prayer book is sovereign; he is worth praying to since he is almighty—transcendent and unsurpassable. On occasion he is also addressed as "Eternal God."[27] But he is also the "Father," the name of God learned from the prayer of Jesus, which features so often in Cranmer's services.[28] The fatherhood of God was a scriptural theme rediscovered in the Reformation. It was a distinctive feature of John Calvin's theological vision, as he expressed it in his *Institutes of the Christian Religion*. And it had a particular significance within his system, as it did for Cranmer: Christians can address God as "Father" because they are his children by adoption in Christ. They have, by the cross of Christ, been welcomed into the family of God.

In the twentieth century, prayer book revisions have frequently altered the terms of address for God, seeking, on the one hand, to minimize the emphasis on the divine power and, on the other, to gender-neutralize the language of "Father." Both of these tendencies are sadly misguided and potentially very dangerous for Christian faith, since prayer to a powerless God is of no comfort at all, and prayer to a God who is not the Father of Jesus Christ is not Christian prayer.

The example from the General Confession also addresses God, third, as Maker, and this order is representative of the whole prayer

25. Ketley, *Two Liturgies*, 90.
26. Compare the General Confession in Morning and Evening Prayer: "Almighty and most merciful Father." Ketley, *Two Liturgies*, 218.
27. See, for example, the prayer in the marriage service: "O Eternal God, creator and preserver of all mankind." Ketley, *Two Liturgies*, 129.
28. See, for example, the Collect for Grace in Morning Prayer: "O Lord, our heavenly Father, almighty and everliving God." Ketley, *Two Liturgies*, 35.

book.[29] There is not a sense that the people are praying simply to the divine clockmaker or the lazy deist divinity of the eighteenth century. He is Creator, but he is known to us as Creator because of his work in salvation history. The narrative of the Bible, and especially of Jesus Christ, is the focal point—the window onto God's nature. He is Father because he is the Father of Jesus, the brother of Christians. He is Father because he is the Father of many prodigal children, whom he welcomes with tender and loving arms back into the fold.

In public prayer, Christians were to pray as they were to do in private: by confessing their sins, by thanking God, by praising him, and by bringing before him their common needs. For example, the exhortation before the General Confession in Morning Prayer reads,

> And although we ought at all times humbly to [acknowledge] our sins before God: yet ought we most chiefly so to do, when we assemble and meet together, to render thanks for the great benefits that we have received at his hands, to set forth his most worthy praise, to hear his most holy word, and to ask those things which be requisite and necessary, as well for the body as the soul.[30]

We shall consider each form of prayer briefly.

CONFESSION

From 1552 onward, the striking thing about the daily services was the prominent place given to the general confession of sins. Henceforth, both Morning and Evening Prayer would begin in this way.[31] The required practice of auricular confession and priestly absolution had been abolished because, it was argued, it placed a mediator other than Christ between the believer and God. But the gospel

---

29. See note 26 above.
30. Ketley, *Two Liturgies*, 218.
31. Ketley, *Two Liturgies*, 217.

of justification by faith is not a declaration that the Christian has moved to a state of sinlessness. Indeed, the basis for the gathering of the Christian church is the shared need of fallen sinners. The act of general confession reminds the congregation of that common need and, indeed, of their assurance of forgiveness, for the confession takes place in the light of the promises of the gospel.

Confession begins with the reading of Scriptures that both remind the congregation of their sins and point to the promises of the merciful Father. First John 1:8–9 is typical of this theme: "If we say we have no sin, we deceive ourselves, and the truth is not in us. If we confess our sins, he is faithful and just to forgive us our sins and to cleanse us from all unrighteousness." The exhortation that follows likewise aims to bring to the notice of the congregants the reality of ongoing sin in their lives and the promises of God in Christ. It enjoins the congregation, "Accompany me with a pure heart and humble voice, unto the throne of the heavenly grace."[32] Thus, the basis of the Christian confession of sin is not fear of punishment but humble expectation of grace.

And thus follows the confession itself, which articulates a thoroughgoing doctrine of sin in the life of the believer.[33] A number of metaphors are used: the straying sheep, the trespasser against the holy laws of God, and sin as sickness ("there is no health in us"). This last expression is a radical statement of the situation before God even of the baptized Christian. There is, by nature, nothing that simply commends the person to God. Always tainted to some degree by our innate self-centeredness, not only our actions but even the "devices and desires of our own hearts" are blameworthy in God's perfect sight. We have an orientation within that is badly askew.

But the prayer turns around the plea for the Lord God to "have mercy upon us miserable offenders" (i.e., people who are in misery because of their sins), as he himself has promised in Christ Jesus. The final petition of the prayer is that the believer might live a

32. Ketley, *Two Liturgies*, 218.
33. Ketley, *Two Liturgies*, 218–19.

"godly, righteous and sober life"—a striking recognition that the changed heart of the believer is the work of God. In Holy Communion, too, the congregational response to the reading of the law is the same in structure: "Lord, have mercy on us, and incline our hearts to keep this law."[34] In fallen human beings, keeping the law of God requires a change of heart brought about only by a work of God. Mercy precedes reform, and not the other way around. It is worth noting, as well, that the declaration of absolution by the minister is not conditioned on doing penance. There is no penitential requirement, nor can there be: grace accomplishes all.

Praise

A great deal of time is given to God's praise in the Book of Common Prayer. At the time of the Reformation the singing of congregational hymns was not yet commonplace in England. But the praises of God were still to be said, or sung by a choir if present. At Morning Prayer, the lengthy *Te Deum Laudamus*—or the alternative to it, *Benedicite, Omnia Opera*—offers a comprehensive spectrum of God's work for praise. In Morning and Evening Prayer, the praise of God is especially a response to hearing the Scriptures read aloud. The *Magnificat* and the *Nunc Dimittis*, taken from Luke's Gospel, are songs that praise God for the revelation of his salvation in Christ. Theologically speaking, these items of praise place the gospel of Jesus Christ at the forefront of the things for which God is to be praised, and they declare the Scriptures to be the word about that salvation.

But, notably, the praises of the people are not viewed as a kind of divine flattery, as if the people were like the prophets of Baal dancing frantically and cutting themselves in order to get the attention of a sleepy divinity. On the contrary: the responses, based on the penitential Psalm 51, make a striking theological statement about praise:

---

34. Ketley, *Two Liturgies*, 266–67.

Priest. O Lord, open thou our lips.
Answer. And our mouth shall shew forth thy praise.[35]

It is God who opens the lips of people in order that they might praise him. If people praise God, it is because he ordains it. Human praise for God is a response to the gracious initiative that God takes in the gospel. It is not designed to trigger that divine movement toward us. That prior movement of God toward us in Christ is the basis on which our sacrifices of praise and thanksgiving are made acceptable to God.

THANKSGIVING

The human complement of divine grace is, as we have seen, the gratitude of faith. It is with thanksgiving that the believer receives the bread and the wine at Holy Communion. Again, we must see this gratitude not as a payment of some kind for what has been given but simply as an expression of the appropriate human response of dependence on God in all things. But, especially, thanksgiving arises in response to the divine grace shown in the death of Christ Jesus for sin. Hence, after the Absolution and the Comfortable Words in the service of Holy Communion, the priest invokes the people:

Priest. Lift up your hearts.
Answer. We lift them up unto the Lord.
Priest. Let us give thanks unto our Lord God.
Answer. It is meet and right so to do.
Priest. It is very meet, right, and our bounden duty, that we
should at all times, and in all places, give thanks unto thee,
O Lord, holy Father, almighty, everlasting God.[36]

It is strange that thanksgiving prayers were not composed for the 1549 and 1552 editions of the Book of Common Prayer. The thanksgivings that appear in the 1662 book were all seventeenth-century

35. Ketley, *Two Liturgies*, 219.
36. Ketley, *Two Liturgies*, 277.

insertions into the text. Most memorable is probably the General Thanksgiving, composed by Bishop Reynolds of Norwich. It is a classic Anglican prayer; it not only expresses thanks but earnestly prays for more gratitude. Those who offer the prayer give "most humble and hearty thanks" as the unworthy servants of the "Father of all mercies." The focus of thanks moves from creation through to redemption in Christ—"for the means of grace, and for the hope of glory." And then comes the crucial shift, as it swings from thanksgiving into petitionary prayer: it prays that the congregation would receive from God a "due sense of all thy mercies" that they would show in heart and mouth and life the gratitude that God's grace deserves. That is, God himself is the source of the thanksgiving his grace rightly engenders. As it is with praise, if thankfulness arises in his people, then it is because of his work in changing them from within.[37]

PETITION

The petitionary prayers in the Book of Common Prayer are certainly one of its remarkable achievements. They fulfill the brief indicated in the homilies, that the Christian's prayers should be heartfelt but also directed by the word of God to the will of God, and that the spiritual need is more serious than the physical, though the latter is not to be ignored. The Litany, for example, pleads with God for mercy and for delivery from all the temptations of this life before it requests protection from physical calamity "in all time of our tribulation, in all time of our wealth, in the hour of death, and in the day of judgment."[38] Such language reflects the often very fearful state of life in the era when these prayers were composed.

The collects, perhaps so called because they formed a kind of summary of the teaching of Scripture that was being read, were listed to accompany the readings for the different days of the year.

---

37. For the full text of this prayer, see F. E. Brightman, *The English Rite*, 2 vols. (London: Rivingtons, 1915), 1:195.

38. Ketley, *Two Liturgies*, 101.

The collects of the Book of Common Prayer came from a variety of sources. Only a few were specially composed for use in post-Reformation services. They were distinguished by their brevity and thus heavily criticized by the Puritans. They follow a shared pattern: opening with an invocation of God according to his attributes and sometimes according to some piece of the narrative of redemption; then stating a doctrine, which grounds the petition that follows; then the petition itself; then an "aspiration," or the desired result of the prayer; and finally the termination, which usually points to the mediation of Jesus Christ.

Criticisms of the Prayer Book Prayers

The ideals expressed in the Book of Common Prayer were not perfectly implemented by any stretch of the imagination. Though they were intended to be more inclusive and participatory about the meeting of God's people, the reality was that in an era of widespread illiteracy and expensive books, most services in the Church of England were a ministerial monologue, with some interjections from choir or curate. The authorized forms of vernacular prayer on the lips of a lackadaisical and mumbling minister could become as alienating as any Latin service. Gerald Bray comments, "Considering that not everyone could read, that relatively few people possessed a copy of the Prayer Book, and that even the clergy did not always know what they were supposed to be doing, it is hardly surprising that this did not work very well."[39] It was hard to see how the principle of heartfelt calling on God through the mediation of Jesus Christ in the power of the Holy Spirit was being achieved by the use of the book.

It was, after all, a book imposed by government decree. For those in the far corners of the British Isles, the imposition of vernacular English was far worse than the Latin it replaced, since it represented the triumph of the English language over local tongues

39. Bray, "Prayer in the English Reformation: Part 2," 35.

such as Cornish. There were violent uprisings as a result in 1549. The very principle that the Reformation had established was being contravened at the same time as it was being implemented. Happily, translation of the prayer book into other languages began very soon after the first publications (Welsh appearing in the 1560s). English was not to become a new Latin.

Those in the Puritan movement (if we may use that rather loose term) who objected to the prayers in the prayer book did so because they did not believe that the repetition of prayers written by someone else could possibly be heartfelt and Spirit-filled. This concern was not, of course, out of keeping with the theology of the homilies, as we have seen: true prayer to the true God cannot be merely the turning of prayer wheels or the muttering of rote-learned words. And to be fair, the prayer book did not provide a remedy to the problem of congregational prayer per se. Nevertheless, the real bone of contention seems to have been far more a matter of differences over what worked best at a practical level than anything substantially theological. The advantage of set prayers is that they are of a consistent theological outlook and cover not simply the personal preferences of those leading the prayers. On the other hand, the spontaneity and heartfelt nature of prayer *extempore* can prove an excellent antidote to the flatness of set prayers. But, really, as with many of the Cranmerian-era reforms, the biggest obstacle was and remains the lack of a well-trained clergy. Without a trained and pious minister, the prayer book prayers simply do not form the watertight defense against theological corruption that they were intended to provide.

The Future of Prayer in Anglicanism

It is not my task here to rehearse the fascinating and complex history of the prayer book and its prayers from the Reformation down to the present time. The Book of Common Prayer has traveled to places and been used among people unknown to its authors. It has been translated and it has been revised. The revision process has been, in a number of places, a very difficult one, owing to the competing requirements of various theological parties within the Anglican Church, and because of the difficulty of finding modern idioms that express Cranmer's meaning. Further complexity is added by the debates over the appropriate address for God.

Another simple reality for the churches of the Anglican Communion is that the goal of a uniformity in public prayer is scarcely attainable today, even if it were desirable. A greater level of interaction with the nonconformist churches has led to a greater familiarity with, and acceptance of, the practice of extemporaneous prayer. In a church with mature and responsible Christian lay leaders, it is surely edifying to those present if prayers offered are of particular relevance for the congregation assembled. The objection that repetition makes for inauthentic prayer can also be overcome by the freshness of prayers composed each week for use along with the best set prayers.

The idea of the set form of service, from which there can be no deviation, as a way of unifying and norming, even controlling, the churches that fellowship together as "Anglican" has long passed. But the theological convictions that underpinned the creation of the Reformation-era liturgies have not lost their relevance. There is still need for the congregation's approach to God to have that distinctive flavor of grace. The people still need to know that they approach the Father not in order to pacify him but in the confidence of their fellowship with the Son as their only mediator. The advantage of the set prayers of the Anglican liturgy is that, at their best, they present a consistent theology of prayer to the triune God. If set prayers are to be abandoned—as they habitually are, especially in evangelical and charismatic churches—then those who lead the congregation in prayer need to learn to pray theologically. The immediacy of extemporaneous prayer is all for naught if the prayers themselves are shallow.

But the debate about the form in which prayers are said is of comparatively little importance. The real urgent need is for a habit of prayer among Christians that reminds them of the identity of the God whom they worship and their own identity before him. This is why the rhythm of confession, thanksgiving, praise, and petition, so brilliantly captured in Cranmer's liturgies, needs to be preserved even as it is translated into new idioms.

Anglicans will continue to pray. In the Global South, if we are to generalize, they will pray to the God and Father of the Lord Jesus Christ in the midst of those who offer prayers to many other deities, who pray by rote or at set times of the day, or who spin prayer wheels or cast spells or hope to win the favor of the divine by the fervency of their pleas. They will pray confidently to a God who is rich in mercy among those who pray with no confidence, and indeed, in fear. In the West, Anglicans will confess their sins in a culture that is schooled in denials; will give thanks to the God in whose hands everything lies, alongside those who trust only in themselves; will praise another for everything, eschewing self-promotion; and will ask God to provide them with what they truly need even when they outwardly seem to need nothing.

CHAPTER 6

Music: The Word in Song

If your Grace command some devout and solemn note to be made thereunto . . . I trust it will much [excite] and stir the hearts of all men unto devotion and godliness: but in mine opinion, the song that shall be made thereunto would not be full of notes, but as near as may be, for every syllable a note; so that it may be sung distinctly and devoutly, as be in the Matins and Evensong, *Venite*, the Hymns, *Te Deum, Benedictus, Magnificat, Nunc dimittis*, and all the Psalms and Versicles.

Cranmer to King Henry VIII, October 7, 1544[1]

And (to the end the people may the better hear) in such places where they do sing, there shall the lessons be sung in a plain tune after the manner of distinct reading: and likewise the Epistle and the Gospel.

Rubric following instruction on how to conclude the two readings from Scripture, 1549 Book of Common Prayer[2]

---

1. Quoted in Henry Jenkyns, ed., *The Remains of Thomas Cranmer*, 4 vols. (Oxford: Oxford University Press, 1833), 1:315–16.

2. Quoted in Joseph Ketley, ed., *Two Liturgies . . . of Edward VI* (Cambridge: Parker Society, 1844), 30.

It is perhaps impossible for contemporary Christians of any tradition to imagine a church service in which congregational singing does not feature prominently. The hymn singing of the evangelical movement since the eighteenth century and the emphasis on singing in the Pentecostal and charismatic movements of the twentieth century have had an unmistakable influence across Western Christianity in all denominations. Certainly, throughout the globe, an ordinary Anglican service these days is expected to feature congregational singing in addition to whatever other music is provided by a choir, orchestra, or band. Now that Anglicanism is a truly global faith and Anglicans in Africa and Asia feel generally less burdened by having to imitate Englishness, music of a local flavor is more likely to feature in the worship of an Anglican community.

The history of music in the Church of England and its sister churches is more complicated than it might seem. Music in Christian worship was certainly a concern of the Anglican Reformers, but they did not pursue congregational hymn singing to the extent that their Continental colleagues did. Furthermore, the choirs of the colleges and cathedrals were maintained through the turmoil of the sixteenth century, partly owing to royal intervention; and so a tradition of choral music persisted within Anglicanism.

We have seen that the Reformation insistence on a theology of the word shaped the belief and practice of worship that subsequently developed. At least that was the intention of those who, like Cranmer and Jewel, played pioneering roles in the development of Reformation Anglicanism. If worship is chiefly a response of gratitude to the work of the almighty and most merciful God on our behalf, and not an attempt to dazzle God with our performance of piety or with our aesthetic brilliance, then should not music in church serve that grateful end? Certainly, it should; but even so, among the European Reformers there was a wide spectrum of opinion as to the usefulness and the place of music in Christian worship.

A long tradition of suspicion of music in Christianity goes back to the concern about the use of musical instruments in the patristic era,[3] and some Reformers had a good deal of sympathy for that opinion. Calvin wanted to confine the power of music in church to the singing of psalms without accompaniment.[4] Zwingli went even further, opposing all instrumental and vocal music in Christian worship.[5] But these were certainly not the only voices. For example, there were pragmatists like Martin Luther who saw music as a great opportunity to disseminate Reformation ideas among the people. Indeed, the success of Reformation hymnody was the impetus for the composition of hymns by Roman Catholic composers in the counter-Reformation.

The Reformation and Church Music in England

A feature of medieval Christianity, as I have already explained, was the careful delineation of duties between the religious and the secular estates. The story of church music in many ways parallels this. In church, music was performed and observed. It was not a corporate activity but one carried out by those trained for it and called to pursue it. The words sung were in Latin. While for many centuries plainsong—singing unaccompanied in unison—was, officially at least, the form prescribed for church music, by the fourteenth and fifteenth centuries, composers had started to introduce complex polyphonic arrangements. Thus the church historian Erik Routley writes, "Medieval hymnody was as professional as the rest of church music."[6]

There is no disputing the beauty of the music that emerged in the late medieval period. Composers like John Taverner (1490–1545), who was appointed to be organist and choirmaster at Christ Church, Oxford, by Cardinal Wolsey in 1526, produced works of

---

3. See Andrew Wilson-Dickson, *The Story of Christian Music: From Gregorian Chants to Black Gospel* (Minneapolis: Fortress, 1992), 28.

4. W. David O. Taylor, "John Calvin and Musical Instruments: A Critical Investigation," *Calvin Theological Journal* 48, no. 2 (2013): 254.

5. Samuel Macauley Jackson, *Huldreich Zwingli: The Reformer of German Switzerland, 1484–1531* (New York: Putnam, 1901), 290–91.

6. Erik Routley and Lionel Dakers, *A Short History of English Church Music*, rev. ed. (London: Mowbray, 1997), 11.

sophistication and splendor. But what was going on theologically in this music? Certainly, it had its critics, the great scholar Erasmus among them.

> In some countries, the whole day is now spent in endless sing-
> ing, yet one worthwhile sermon exciting true piety is hardly
> heard in six months . . . not to mention the kind of music that has
> been brought into divine worship, in which not a single word
> can be clearly understood. . . . These activities are so pleasing to
> monks, especially the English, that they perform nothing else.[7]

If the words were not understood, then in what sense could it be said that the singing was edifying the hearers? It could be argued that they were hearing uplifting music and experiencing a kind of sacramental blessing as a result. But such an argument did not rest on particularly strong theological or scriptural foundations.

As we have seen, the Reformation view of worship stemmed from its doctrine of justification by faith. This in turn led to an emphasis on vernacular language and the comprehensibility of the words used in church—for if justification is by faith, and faith comes by hearing, then what is said or sung in church must be understand-able by those in attendance. There was also an end to the profes-sionalization of worship—and this had an impact on the music sung by trained monastic choirs. The dissolution of the monasteries in the 1530s under Henry VIII was the end to much of the music that had flourished up until then. But Henry was also a great sponsor of fine music; and so the Chapel Royal continued to house a cultivated form of choral music. In the latter half of the sixteenth century, despite all that was going on in the parishes of England, composers like Thomas Tallis and William Byrd still produced elaborate musi-cal settings for use in worship.

On the Continent, the Reformation led to a variety of approaches to music. Lutheran churches continued to use chants, but also sang

---

7. Andrew G. Shead, "Is There a Musical Note in the Body? Cranmer on the Reformation of Music," *Reformed Theological Review* 69, no. 1 (2010): 2.

congregational hymns—a number of which Luther himself apparently penned. In the Swiss and South German Reformation cities, the preference was for congregationally sung psalms. In Zwingli's Zurich, even though Zwingli himself was a musician, music was ceased altogether.[8] The organ in the Grossmünster was destroyed! If the English Reformation was more cautious than this, however, it was not because the principles of worship established in the theology of the Reformation were somehow being watered down. There was, if anything, an attempt to adapt such music as was available to the new principles of intelligibility and accessibility. Even as early as 1544, Cranmer wrote to Henry:

> If your Grace command some devout and solemn note to be made thereunto . . . I trust it will much [excite] and stir the hearts of all men unto devotion and godliness: but in mine opinion, the song that shall be made thereunto would not be full of notes, but as near as may be, for every syllable a note; so that it may be sung distinctly and devoutly, as be in the Matins and Evensong, *Venite*, the Hymns, *Te Deum, Benedictus, Magnificat, Nunc dimittis*, and all the Psalms and Versicles.[9]

Cranmer was acknowledging the positive effect that music certainly can have on the emotions—to "[excite] and stir the hearts of all men unto devotion and godliness." But he was pleading for fewer notes: too many notes drew attention not to the words but to the music as a channel of access to the divine. "For every syllable a note," requests Cranmer. Why? Because the words need to be sung "distinctly and devoutly." This is in keeping with his emphasis on edification as the purpose of worship, and it also is in keeping with his view of the sacraments and of prayer. You cannot lift your heart to heaven if you cannot understand what you are doing. Too easily people forget the structure of true Christian worship and assume

---

8. Robin A. Leaver, "The Prayer Book 'Noted,'" in *The Oxford Guide to the Book of Common Prayer: A Worldwide Survey*, ed. Charles C. Hefling and Cynthia L. Shattuck (Oxford: Oxford University Press, 2006), 39.

9. Jenkyns, *Remains of Cranmer*, 1:315–16.

that their approach to God is made independently of God's approach to us in Jesus Christ. Cranmer's advice was taken into consideration by composers such as John Marbeck and Thomas Tallis, who both offered compositions in the "every syllable a note" style, even though they did not eschew polyphony. Marbeck's attempt to set the Book of Common Prayer to plainchant, while not an aesthetic masterpiece, was indicative at least that the Reformation theology could perhaps be married to a more "serious" musical form.[10]

But Cranmer himself was no particular fan of choral music if it was a substitute for congregational involvement. The revision of the prayer book in 1552 is notable for the absence of the musical directions that had featured in 1549. In that rite, the choir was given a very prominent place, though restricted mainly to singing passages from Scripture. In 1552, on the other hand, the congregation had replaced them. For example, we may immediately note that "Evensong" became "Evening Prayer."[11] The rubric introducing the new general confession for the daily offices ordered that it "be said of the whole congregation after the minister." Furthermore, the creed in Holy Communion came from the lips of the congregation, whereas in 1549 the instruction was that "the Clerks shall sing."[12] Andrew Shead of Moore College explains, "It was not singing per se that he worked to eliminate from services, but choral singing that excluded the people."[13]

But what kind of congregational singing did Cranmer envisage? The group of Cambridge scholars that first advocated Lutheran teaching in England was clearly impressed by Luther's use of music to disseminate his ideas. George Joye published translations of Luther's hymns as early as 1527. In 1535, Miles Coverdale, better known for his translation of the Bible, produced a work entitled *Goostly Psalms and Spirituall Songs drawen out of the holy Scripture, for the*

10. See Eric Hunt, ed., *Cranmer's First Litany, 1544, and Merbecke's Book of Common Prayer Noted, 1550* (London: SPCK, 1939).
11. Shead, "Is There a Musical Note?," 6.
12. Ketley, *Two Liturgies*, 78, 218, 224–25, 268.
13. Shead, "Is There a Musical Note?," 6.

comforte and consolacyon of soch as loue to reioyse in God and his worde. This volume contained forty-one hymns, including several by Luther, intended for unaccompanied congregational singing, as in the German churches. When *Goostly Psalms* was published, there was no thought of it becoming a hymn book for use in public services; but it clearly had an impact, since Henry VIII ordered that copies of it be burned in 1546. In 1544, Cranmer himself tried his hand as a hymn writer and translator, although he was not altogether pleased with the result.[14] In the following year, the "King and his clergy" set forth an official primer that was to replace all others as the new standard for lay devotion at home and privately in church during the Latin Mass.[15] The primer of 1545 offered a number of reworked and translated hymns with the intention that the laity could sing God's praises in their own language. Finally, once permission had been given for the use of the vernacular in church under Edward's reign, the composition of metrical translations of psalms became widespread.

We may fairly assume, then, that Cranmer was not opposed to the use of music in church but, in particular, supported the singing of psalms and canticles by the congregation, with or without the aid of a choir. The emphasis was on metrical translations of passages of Scripture rather than on freshly composed hymns, and on the intelligibility of the words sung. Elizabeth I herself gave approval for congregational singing of psalms and hymns in the Royal Injunctions of 1559:

... that there be a modest and distinct song, so used in all parts of the Common Prayers in the Church, that the same may be plainly [understood], as if it were read without singing. And yet,

---

14. "As concerning the *Salve festa dies* ... wherefore I have travailed to make the verses in English ... by cause mine English verses lack the grace and facility that I would wish they had, your Majesty may cause some other to make them again, that can do the same in more pleasant English and phrase." Jenkyns, *Remains of Cranmer*, 1:316.

15. For the text of this primer, see *The Primer Set Foorth by the Kynges Maistie and His Clergie (1545)* (Charleston: Eebo Editions, 2010). For an analysis of its contents, see Charles C. Butterworth, *The English Primers (1529–1545): Their Publication and Connection with the English Bible and the Reformation in England* (Philadelphia: University of Pennsylvania Press, 1953), 256–75.

nevertheless, for the comforting of such as delight in music, it
may be permitted, that in the beginning, or in the end of Common Prayers, either at morning or evening, there may be sung
an hymn, or such-like song, to the praise of Almighty God, in
the best sort of melody and music that may be conveniently
devised, having respect that the sentence of the hymn may be
[understood] and perceived.[16]

In 1560, John Jewel wrote to Peter Martyr on how the practice
had already spread like wildfire:

Religion is now somewhat more established than it was. The
people are every where exceedingly inclined to the better part.
The practice of joining in church music has very much con-
duced to this. For as soon as they had once commenced singing
in public, in only one little church in London, immediately not
only the churches in the neighbourhood, but even the towns
far distant, began to view with each other in the same practice.
You may now sometimes see at Paul's cross,[17] after the service,
six thousand persons, old and young, of both sexes, all singing
together and praising God.[18]

Even if we allow for a little exaggeration in this account, it
stands as evidence that the practice of congregational singing had
taken hold in England at the early part of Elizabeth's reign, just as
it had on the Continent.

The Music of the Cathedrals

One of the great paradoxes of the English church is the way the
cathedral choir tradition persisted even while something quite
different was going on in the parish churches.[19] Historically, it is

---

16. W. H. Frere and W. P. M. Kennedy, eds., *Visitation Articles and Injunctions of the Period
of the Reformation, 1536–1575*, 3 vols. (London: Longmans Green, 1910), 3:23.

17. The outdoor preaching pulpit of St Paul's Cathedral, London.

18. Hastings Robinson, ed., *The Zurich Letters... during the Early Part of the Reign of Queen
Elizabeth* (Cambridge: Parker Society, 1842), 71.

19. This is not the place for a full history of English cathedral music, several histories of
which have been written. See Kenneth Roy Long, *The Music of the English Church* (London:

not difficult to make sense of this: the preference of royalty for the fine art of the choral tradition meant that the cathedral choirs were a protected species. But the kind of theological shift that led to changes in the parish churches did not seem to impact the music of the cathedrals to the same degree. The music of the cathedrals drew the ire of the Puritans in the seventeenth century, but was revived in the restoration of the monarchy in 1660. Cranmer's insistence on "one note per syllable" was readily forgotten, and an increasingly sophisticated music was on offer.

Puritan critics like William Prynne felt that the music of the cathedrals was evidence of a return to Romish ways.[20] Certainly, the self-conscious step away from the tenets of the Reformation found in churchmen such as William Laud and Lancelot Andrewes became associated with a renewed emphasis on the aesthetic in worship, and with the Catholic sympathies of Charles I and his French wife, Henrietta. One should perhaps not blame musicians for this: musicians will tend to compose and make music in whatever conditions they are permitted to operate. Nevertheless, commentators often note the disparity between cathedral music and the music of regular worship in the parish church as evidence of separate traditions.[21]

The contrast became even more apparent with the rise of hymn singing during the evangelical movement of the eighteenth and nineteenth centuries. Previously, metrical psalms had been the staple fare of the Sunday service. But the Wesleys (John and Charles) and the other leading lights of the evangelical movement encouraged hymn singing in their midweek and open-air meetings. The Olney hymns, written for use in the parish church and published in

Hodder & Stoughton, 1972); Routley and Dakers, *Short History of English Church Music*; and, best of all, Andrew Gant, *O Sing unto the Lord: A History of English Church Music* (Chicago: University of Chicago Press, 2017).

20. Peter Le Huray, *Music and the Reformation in England, 1549–1660*, Cambridge Studies in Music (Cambridge: Cambridge University Press, 1978), 52.

21. For the changing nature of worship practices in post-Reformation England, see Kenneth Fincham and Nicholas Tyacke, *Altars Restored: The Changing Face of English Religious Worship, 1547–c. 1700* (Oxford: Oxford University Press, 2007).

1779 by poet William Cowper and his friend John Newton, curate of the parish church, were an instant success. The Cambridge evangelical leader Charles Simeon published his own volume of hymns: *A Collection of Psalms and Hymns from Various Authors, Chiefly Designed for the Use of Public Worship.* The title itself shows that the practice of singing hymns in church was a regular feature in parish churches at least. Yet, until the early nineteenth century, many regular Church of England congregations would not venture singing at Morning and Evening Prayer hymns that were not direct translations or versifications of Scripture. Many thought the practice illegal (it wasn't). But once it began, the practice became widespread. The leaders of the Anglo-Catholic movement, originally skeptical of the new fashion for hymn singing, quickly ascertained that it was a practice of the ancient church and adopted it wholeheartedly. More than 250 hymnals were published in the nineteenth century before the magisterial *Hymns Ancient and Modern* swept all before it.[22] Today, there is now far more congregational singing of all sorts in Anglican church services than ever before.

For its part, the cathedral tradition has persisted and certainly flourished in the last two centuries—in England and elsewhere. There was in the twentieth century a renewal of the choral tradition, with much fine new music composed by Herbert Howells, Gustav Holst, Benjamin Britten, and Ralph Vaughan Williams, to name but a few. The choral music of the cathedrals at its best aspires to the finest of fine arts.

However, is the music of the cathedrals the embodiment of a different theology of worship than that of the Reformation Anglicanism that has concerned us in this book? It certainly can be. One of the ongoing difficulties for theological reflection in this matter is that cathedral musicians have understandably not produced much by way of a sustained theological account of worship to accompany their practice of worship. Kenneth R. Long's *The Music of the En-*

glish Church is a case in point. Long is wonderfully erudite about the history of choral and congregational music. But his theological statements are mostly given as opinionated asides. In justifying the expense of maintaining a cathedral's worship, he writes:

> Those who inveigh against the immense cost of maintaining daily choral services might well remember the disciples' question 'To what purpose is this waste? For this ointment might have been sold for much and given to the poor.' Our Lord's stern rebuke on that occasion shows the value he placed on an act of pure worship, however costly. Good-neighbourliness must never become a substitute for true worship—and there is always an element of sacrifice in worship. The daily round of choral services, morning as well as evening, in the mother church of the diocese is a unique and continuing act of worship—whether any congregation is present or not. It is beside the point that many who do come experience an inspiration and an access of spiritual power which no other form of worship can bring them.[23]

This is, to put a finer point on it, simply paganism. It reflects no principles of a genuine Christian theology whatsoever and echoes the days before the Reformation when the business of divine worship was outsourced to professionals. As I have sought to explain in this book, a theology of true worship is not, in the first instance, about the making of sacrifices to God.

There are five problems with Long's statement. First, true worship begins with the action of God toward us in Christ—for Jesus Christ is the one who offers true worship to the Father on behalf of all humanity. Second, our involvement in Christ's true worship is certainly inclusive of "good neighborliness"—the adoration of God on its own is a kind of blasphemy without the works that match it. Third, though the New Testament does use the language of sacrifice for our acts of response to the primary and atoning sacrifice of

---

23. Long, *Music of the English Church*, 387–88.

Christ upon the cross, the danger of this language out of context is that it sounds like a system of merit—which is total anathema to the Reformation gospel. Fourth, the idea of the singing of God's praises with no congregation present in no way resembles any New Testament view of the gathering of the church as it praises the Father. What we might call the "vertical" aspect of meeting together as God's people is incomprehensible if they are not actually gathered. The praises of God go together with the edification of his people: without one, the other is not what it is supposed to be. Fifth, while for some people choral music has a particular significance and effect ("an access of spiritual power"), the Reformation understanding of the work of the Spirit of God ties it to the word of God. That is not to say that the word of God is presented in the sermon or readings only. Not at all: the sacraments are a different mode in which the word may be spoken. The word of God, as Cranmer saw, can also be presented in the form of music. But it is not the aesthetic effect of the music that has the "spiritual power": it is the word of God by the power of the Spirit of God that has that effect.

In Reformation thought, aestheticism is not in itself a channel of grace. The "splendor of holiness" (Ps. 96:9) has too often been interpreted as "the holiness of beauty." That is part of the Reformation protest. As with any art, the great aesthetic charm of fine music is not in and of itself sacramental. Beauty itself may be a complete distraction from the gospel of Jesus Christ, who, after all, "had . . . no beauty" (Isa. 53:2). The smashing of the statues and the painting over of the images in the sixteenth century (an episode repeated in the seventeenth) was evidence not of philistinism (as it is so often portrayed today) but of a horror that the true word of God and the right way to worship the God who speaks in his word were being obscured by religious bric-a-brac. Likewise, the protest against a music that is not the servant of the gospel of Jesus Christ—but appears to be an end in itself—is not simply an instance of tone deafness but springs from a genuinely Christian conviction about the true worship of God.

But there was—and is—another way. In Germany, Luther did not resort to iconoclasm but instead adapted what he found to gospel purposes. In England, Cranmer evinced a commitment to a similar principle. He adapted the rites and ceremonies of the pre-Reformation English church, retrofitting them to match the Reformation gospel. His question was *Can it be used for the gospel?* As we have seen, this did not mean that he left liturgy and music unaltered. He had some quite specific things to say about the music of the church. And, yet, he did not object in principle to choral music but felt that it could certainly become a vehicle for true religion. As Jaroslav Pelikan has shown, the extraordinary music of Johann Sebastian Bach was a reflection on distinctively Lutheran theological themes.[24] Could not the same be true of the tradition of Anglican choral music—that, with the right theological understanding of the function of music in Christian worship, it could adorn the evangelical gospel?

The fine music of the choirs need not be anathema to the principles of Reformation Anglican worship, if it adorns the word of God and the Reformation understanding of faith. It is meet and right that God's praises be sung by God's people. That an art form has developed for the very purpose of doing this is a blessing. Choral music has emerged as a style found nowhere else. As with gospel music and hymn singing, it is the church's own. If the children of the 1960s rejected traditional Anglican music as too distant from the massive changes in popular music they enthusiastically supported, the current generation of millennials is seeking the exact opposite— to be rooted in something that transcends contemporary culture. This new reality gives the Anglican heritage of sacred music a missional edge in alluring younger people back into the fold.

Music and Reformation Anglican Worship Today

The same tension that the Reformers faced between performance-art music and music by and for the people exists in Anglican

---

24. Jaroslav Pelikan, *Bach among the Theologians* (Philadelphia: Fortress, 1986).

churches today. Surprisingly, perhaps, this is true in contemporary styles of worship as much as in traditional styles. Influenced by Pentecostal and charismatic music, many Anglican churches have both developed a contemporary "folk" style *and* reverted to a more musician-centered form of music, to which quality and volume are central. The musicians now occupy even the place where once the holy table stood, with the drum kit becoming the permanent feature of some church furniture. Andrew Gant writes:

> The "worship band" is here to stay. It has proved itself the ideal musical vehicle for Evangelical congregational worship since its introduction in the early 1970s, being approachable and adaptable, with the early preference for acoustic instruments and a folk style mostly giving way to amplified rock.[25]

He continues, "There is an irony here that the strand of ecclesiology which set out to remove the impression of a separate group of musicians giving a 'performance' has ended up with exactly that: a worship leader with a microphone, facing the 'audience,' his backing musicians behind him, like any other gig."[26]

Gant's point is well made. In many churches of the evangelical and charismatic traditions, music has taken the place of liturgy almost entirely. There is no saying of any words together beyond the sung choruses. The gathering is mostly a combination of singing and sermon. In the era of increasing secularization and the loss of a cultural memory of the classic hymns of generations past, many churches seek to replicate in sound and quality the music of the culture around them, so that visitors feel comfortable and engaged. However, in an era of widespread access to professional music, this is harder and harder to manage effectively. We live in an age with a glut of beautiful sounds, and the church musician is now playing for an audience used to the finest recordings of music available. How can an amateur musician compete with that? When

---

25. Gant, *O Sing unto the Lord*, 360.
26. Gant, *O Sing unto the Lord*, 360.

a church is blessed with professional-level talent, the talent often takes center stage.

There is nothing necessarily wrong with the replacement of said responses by contemporary songs. On the contrary—effective congregational music may be used to edify the congregation in just the way that Cranmer intended. Cranmer was, as we have seen, remarkably pragmatic about matters of style and envisaged times and places in which forms of worship would diverge. However, it takes effective and thoughtful work from pastors and musicians to make sure that they do not simply rotate the congregation's favorites but do seek to take worshipers on the kind of liturgical journey that the Book of Common Prayer does. Contemporary music can tend to emphasize a single emotional moment in the Christian experience rather than the full range, from sorrowful repentance to joyous hope.

Musical style is interesting, and certainly people care very deeply about it. Churches are probably divided more over styles of music than they are over theological questions. The style of music we are greeted with in church can speak to the dearest places in our hearts or be absolutely unbearable. But, ultimately, musical style should be a mostly irrelevant question for consideration in church music. In principle, any instrument and any style could feature in an authentically Anglican service. However, church music must serve the word of God and edify the people. It cannot obscure the word or draw attention to its own beauty, lest we worship it instead. Does the music of the contemporary Anglican church serve the purpose of letting "the word of Christ dwell in you richly"? That must be the question foremost in the minds of today's Anglican musicians, whether they are leading robed choirs or plugged-in worship bands.

Acknowledgments

This book, though not lengthy, has had a long gestation. It began with a truly memorable writers' retreat at "The Hookses," the late John Stott's retreat in Pembrokeshire, in 2012. The group that assembled included the Most Reverend Dr. Benjamin A. Kwashi, the Right Reverend Dr. Michael Nazir-Ali, the Reverend Dr. John W. Yates III, and the Reverend Canon Dr. Ashley J. Null. With prayer and conversation, we committed ourselves to this project and committed the project into God's hands. I should like to thank that group for their counsel and friendship, especially John and Ashley. Ashley Null is that rare combination of a genuine scholar, with an eye for the minutest detail, and a pastor and evangelist. Co-teaching with him at Moore Theological College and subsequently hosting him as a preacher at St Mark's Darling Point have been real privileges.

I should like to give my thanks to the parish where I serve as rector—St Mark's Darling Point. I left academia in part because I wanted the experience of leading a congregation shaped by Cranmer's words in the 1662 Book of Common Prayer. It has been a deep blessing to me as an Anglican born after the liturgical revisions of the 1960s and 1970s (and so a "non-native" to the prayer book) to worship the Lord Jesus week in and week out in the words shaped by Cranmer. Dr. William Clark, the director of music at St Mark's, has been an invaluable colleague and guide.

I should also like to thank my father, the Right Reverend Dr. Peter F. Jensen, for his example of Cranmerian spirituality—his dedication to living under the word of God in prayerful gratitude. To see him at his prayers in his study each morning was an experience I am coming to appreciate more as year succeeds year.

Lastly, thanks to my dear family—to Simon, who helped with some proofreading, and to Sacha, Matilda, and Freya; and, of course, to Catherine, whose patience is inestimable.

Bibliography

À Kempis, Thomas. *The Imitation of Christ*. Peabody, MA: Hendrickson, 2004.

Anglican Church of Canada. *The Book of Alternative Services of the Anglican Church of Canada*. Toronto: Anglican Book Centre, 1985.

Augustine. *Questions on the Heptateuch*. Bk. 3.

Bainton, Roland, H. *Here I Stand: A Life of Martin Luther*. Peabody, MA: Hendrickson, 2009.

Balthasar, Hans Urs von. *The Glory of the Lord*. Vol. 5, *The Realm of Metaphysics in the Modern Age*. Cambridge: Cambridge University Press, 2001.

Bray, Gerald. "Prayer in the English Reformation: Part 1." *Credo* 4, no. 4 (2014): 24–31.

Bray, Gerald. "Prayer in the English Reformation: Part 2." *Credo* 4, no. 4 (2014): 32–41.

Brightman, F. E. *The English Rite*. 2 vols. London: Rivingtons, 1915.

Butterworth, Charles C. *The English Primers (1529–1545): Their Publication and Connection with the English Bible and the Reformation in England*. Philadelphia: University of Pennsylvania Press, 1953.

Calvin, John. *Institutes of the Christian Religion*. Translated by Henry Beveridge. Edited by Henry Beveridge. Rev. ed. Peabody, MA: Hendrickson, 2008.

Carnley, Peter. *Reflections in Glass: Trends and Tensions in the Contemporary Anglican Church*. Pymble, NSW: HarperCollins, 2004.

Carson, D. A., and World Evangelical Fellowship. *Worship: Adoration and Action*. Grand Rapids, MI: Baker, 1993.

Chapman, Mark D. *Anglican Theology*. London: T&T Clark, 2012.

Colclough, David, ed. *Oxford Edition of the Sermons of John Donne*. Vol. 3, *Sermons Preached at the Court of Charles I*. Oxford: Oxford University Press, 2013.

Corrie, George Elwes, ed. *Sermons by Hugh Latimer*. Cambridge: Parker Society, 1844.

Dix, Gregory. *The Shape of the Liturgy*. 2nd ed. London: Continuum, 2001.

Donne, John. "Batter My Heart," Holy Sonnet 14.

Duffy, Eamon. *The Stripping of the Altars: Traditional Religion in England, c. 1400–c. 1580*. New Haven, CT: Yale University Press, 1992. 2nd ed., 2005.

Fincham, Kenneth, and Nicholas Tyacke. *Altars Restored: The Changing Face of English Religious Worship, 1547–c. 1700*. Oxford: Oxford University Press, 2007.

Frere, W. H., and W. P. M. Kennedy, eds. *Visitation Articles and Injunctions of the Period of the Reformation, 1536–1575*. London: Longmans Green, 1910.

Gant, Andrew. *O Sing unto the Lord: A History of English Church Music*. Chicago: University of Chicago Press, 2017.

Gee, Henry, and William John Hardy. *Documents Illustrative of English Church History*. London: Macmillan, 1896.

Griffiths, John. *Two Books of Homilies*. Oxford: Oxford University Press, 1859.

Grosart, A. B., ed. *The Poetical Works of George Herbert*. London: George Bell, 1886.

Hardwick, Charles. *A History of the Articles of Religion*. Cambridge: Deighton Bell, 1859.

Hefling, Charles C. "Introduction: Anglicans and Common Prayer." In *The Oxford Guide to the Book of Common Prayer: A Worldwide Survey*, edited by Charles C. Hefling and Cynthia L. Shattuck, 1–8. Oxford: Oxford University Press, 2006.

Hooker, Richard. *Of the Laws of Ecclesiastical Polity*. Edited by Arthur Stephen McGrade. Cambridge: Cambridge University Press, 1989.

Howe, John W., and Samuel C. Pascoe. *Our Anglican Heritage: Can an Ancient Church Be a Church of the Future?* 2nd ed. Eugene, OR: Cascade, 2010.

Hunt, Eric, ed. *Cranmer's First Litany, 1544, and Merbecke's Book of Common Prayer Noted, 1550.* London: SPCK, 1939.

Jackson, Samuel Macauley. *Huldreich Zwingli: The Reformer of German Switzerland, 1484–1531.* New York: Putnam, 1901.

James, William. *The Varieties of Religious Experience: A Study in Human Nature.* New York: Modern Library, 1994.

Jeanes, Gordon. "Cranmer and Common Prayer." In *The Oxford Guide to the Book of Common Prayer: A Worldwide Survey,* edited by Charles C. Hefling and Cynthia L. Shattuck, 21–38. Oxford: Oxford University Press, 2006.

Jenkyns, Henry, ed. *The Remains of Thomas Cranmer.* 4 vols. Oxford: Oxford University Press, 1833.

Jensen, Michael. "'Simply' Reading the Geneva Bible: The Geneva Bible and Its Readers." *Literature and Theology* 9, no. 1 (1995): 30–45.

Keble, John, ed. *The Works of That Learned and Judicious Divine, Mr. Richard Hooker: Containing Eight Books of the Laws of Ecclesiastical Polity, and Several Other Treatises; with an Index to the Whole. To Which Is Prefixed the Life of the Author by Isaac Walton.* Edited by Arthur Stephen McGrade. 7th ed. 3 vols. Oxford: Clarendon, 1888.

Ketley, Joseph, ed. *The Two Liturgies . . . in the Reign of King Edward the Sixth.* Cambridge: Parker Society, 1844.

Leaver, Robin A. "The Prayer Book 'Noted.'" In *The Oxford Guide to the Book of Common Prayer: A Worldwide Survey,* edited by Charles C. Hefling and Cynthia L. Shattuck, 39–43. Oxford: Oxford University Press, 2006.

Lehmann, Helmut T., and Martin E. Lehmann, eds. *Luther's Works.* Vol. 38, *Word and Sacrament IV.* Philadelphia: Fortress, 1971.

Le Huray, Peter. *Music and the Reformation in England, 1549–1660.* Cambridge Studies in Music. Cambridge: Cambridge University Press, 1978.

Lloyd, Charles. *Formularies of Faith Put Forth by Authority during the Reign of Henry VIII.* Oxford: Oxford University Press, 1856.

Long, Kenneth Roy. *The Music of the English Church.* London: Hodder & Stoughton, 1972.

MacCulloch, Diarmaid. *The Later Reformation in England, 1547–1603.* 2nd ed. Basingstoke: Palgrave, 2001.

MacCulloch, Diarmaid. *Thomas Cranmer: A Life*. New Haven, CT: Yale University Press, 1996.

Marshall, Peter. *Beliefs and the Dead in Reformation England*. Oxford: Oxford University Press, 2002.

Neil, Charles, and J. M. Willoughby. *The Tutorial Prayerbook*. London: Harrison Trust, 1912.

Null, Ashley. "Cranmer's Reputation Reconsidered." In *Reformation Reputations*, edited by David Crankshaw and George Gross. London: Palgrave Macmillan, forthcoming.

Null, Ashley. "Official Tudor Homilies." In *The Oxford Handbook of the Early Modern Sermon*, edited by Peter E. McCullough, Hugh Adlington, and Emma Rhatigan, 348–59. Oxford: Oxford University Press, 2011.

Null, Ashley. *Thomas Cranmer's Doctrine of Repentance: Renewing the Power to Love*. Oxford: Oxford University Press, 2000.

O'Donovan, Oliver. *On the Thirty Nine Articles: A Conversation with Tudor Christianity*. 2nd ed. Exeter: Paternoster, 2011.

Old, Hughes Oliphant. *The Reading and Preaching of the Scriptures in the Worship of the Christian Church*. 7 vols. Grand Rapids, MI: Eerdmans, 2002.

Pelikan, Jaroslav. *Bach among the Theologians*. Philadelphia: Fortress, 1986.

Peterson, David. *Engaging with God: A Biblical Theology of Worship*. Leicester: Apollos, 1992.

Robinson, Hastings, ed. *The Zurich Letters . . . during the Early Part of the Reign of Queen Elizabeth*. Cambridge: Parker Society, 1842.

Routley, Erik, and Lionel Dakers. *A Short History of English Church Music*. Rev. ed. London: Mowbray, 1997.

Ryle, John Charles. *Knots Untied*. 10th ed. London: Thynne, 1898.

Seaver, Paul S. *The Puritan Lectureships: The Politics of Religious Dissent, 1560–1662*. Stanford, CA: Stanford University Press, 1970.

Shead, Andrew G. "Is There a Musical Note in the Body? Cranmer on the Reformation of Music." *Reformed Theological Review* 69, no. 1 (2010): 1–16.

Stott, John R. W. *I Believe in Preaching*. London: Hodder & Stoughton, 1982.

Taylor, W. David O. "John Calvin and Musical Instruments: A Critical Investigation." *Calvin Theological Journal* 48, no. 2 (2013): 248–69.

Torrance, James. *Worship, Community, and the Triune God of Grace.* Didsbury Lectures. Carlisle: Paternoster, 1996.

Tyndale, William, and David Daniell. *The Obedience of a Christian Man.* Penguin Classics. New York: Penguin, 2000.

Wabuda, Susan. *Preaching during the English Reformation.* Cambridge: Cambridge University Press, 2002.

Walter, Henry, ed. *Doctrinal Treatises . . . by William Tyndale.* Cambridge: Parker Society, 1848.

Wannenwetsch, Bernd, and Margaret Kohl. *Political Worship: Ethics for Christian Citizens.* Oxford: Oxford University Press, 2004.

Ware, Bruce A. "The Meaning of the Lord's Supper in the Theology of Ulrich Zwingli (1484–1531)." In *The Lord's Supper: Remembering and Proclaiming Christ Until He Comes*, edited by Thomas R. Schreiner and Matthew R. Crawford, 229–47. Nashville: B&H, 2010.

Webster, J. B. *Holy Scripture: A Dogmatic Sketch.* Cambridge: Cambridge University Press, 2003.

White, James F. "Prayer Book Architecture." In *The Oxford Guide to the Book of Common Prayer: A Worldwide Survey*, edited by Charles C. Hefling and Cynthia L. Shattuck, 106–15. Oxford: Oxford University Press, 2006.

Wilson-Dickson, Andrew. *The Story of Christian Music: From Gregorian Chants to Black Gospel.* Minneapolis: Fortress, 1992.

Wooding, Lucy. "From Tudor Humanism to Reformation Preaching." In *The Oxford Handbook of the Early Modern Sermon*, edited by Peter E. McCullough, Hugh Adlington, and Emma Rhatigan, 329–47. Oxford: Oxford University Press, 2011.

General Index

Abraham, 32, 102
absolution, 64–66
Adonai, 26n4
aestheticism, 165, 168
affections, 74
alb, 70
altar, 67, 126
Anabaptists, 104, 117
Andrewes, Lancelot, 165
Anglican identity, 15
Anglican preaching, 76
Anglican worship
  diversity in, 14
  as sacramental, 107–8
  theological principles of, 14
  unity in, 13
Anglo-Catholic movement, 14, 166
apophatic tradition in Christianity, 96
Articles of Religion, 16
  Article 6, 100, 101
  Article 20, 98
  Article 25, 112
  Article 28, 127
  Article 31, 112
  Article 34, 13–14
Atkinson, Rowan, 76
atonement, 43, 141
Augustine, 56, 108, 141, 143
auricular confession, 64, 148

Bach, Johann Sebastian, 169
Balaam, 28

Balthasar, Hans Urs von, 139–40
baptism, 21, 117–22
baptismal regeneration, 120–21, 132
Barnes, Robert, 77
Basil, 145
"believer's baptism," 117
Benedicite, Omnia Opera, 150
Beza, 69
Bilney, Thomas, 77
Bishops' Bible, 91
Bishops' Book (1537), 111
Black Rubric, 67, 70
body motif, 46
Book of Common Prayer
  absolutions in, 64–65
  ambiguity in, 15–16
  on ceremonies, 51, 61–62
  changes in address to God, 21
  criticisms of prayers in, 153–54
  as feast of Scripture, 66, 88–90
  form and theology of, 74
  and mid-sixteenth-century England, 52
  as missional document, 74
  as political document, 74
  prayer in, 137, 145–53
  on sacraments, 66–68
  updating and translating of, 13, 154
Book of Common Prayer (1549), 12, 51, 61–64, 70, 88, 151, 157, 162
Book of Common Prayer (1552), 12, 64–65, 70, 151, 162

Day of Atonement, 35, 41
Derrida, Jacques, 96
Devotio Moderna, 139
divine initiative and human response, in worship, 31
Dix, Dom Gregory, 68
Donne, John, 84
Duffy, Eamon, 53, 60

eating the word, 86–87, 100
edification, 47–48, 52, 64, 73, 145, 168, 171
Edward VI, King, 11, 68, 77, 114
elevating the host, 132
Elijah, and priests of Baal, 26
Elizabeth I, Queen, 16, 69–70, 163
Elizabethan Settlement, 68–73
Elohim, 26n4
England, as unploughed ground, 79
English Bible, 75, 90–91
English Reformation, 51, 58–60
and prayer in the vernacular, 136
Erasmian humanism, 60, 85
Erasmus, 57, 75, 83–84, 139, 160
eschatology, of worship, 47
European humanism, 83–84
exhortation, 103
existential experience, 43
ex opere operato, 109, 117
expository preaching, 106
extemporaneous prayers, 154, 155

faith
cognitive aspect of, 80
from hearing the word, 57–58, 78
false worship, 24–31
famine of the word of God, 101
"Father," gender-neutralized language for, 147
fear of the Lord, 36–37
Fisher, John, 75, 83
forgiveness of sins, 64–65
Forty-Two Articles. *See* Articles of Religion
Foucault, Michel, 96

Gant, Andrew, 170
Gardiner, Stephen, 116
General Confession (Book of Common Prayer), 146, 147, 148
Geneva Bible, 91
gifts of the Spirit, 47
Global South, prayer in, 156
Gnosticism, 97
God
as "Eternal God," 147
as "Father," 147
as God who speaks, 96–98
jealousy of, 29
as Maker, 147–48
sovereignty of, 147
transcendence of, 97, 147
good works, 74
Goostly Psalms and Spirituall Songs drawen out of the holy Scripture (Coverdale), 162–63
Gorham, George, 120
gospel, and worship, 19
Gothic Revival, 93
grace, 122, 150
and Christian worship, 73
double meaning of, 41
Great Bible, 59, 90, 91
Gregory of Nazianzus, 96
Groote, Geert, 139
Gueranger, Prosper, 17

habit of prayer, 155–56
Harnack, Adolf von, 43
hearing church, 92, 103
Hefling, Charles, 20
Henry VIII, King, 12, 53, 58–60, 90, 111, 163
Herbert, George, 135
Hick, John, 43
high priest, 41
Holst, Gustav, 166
Holy Spirit, 42, 84
gifts of, 47
presence in Lord's Supper, 115
and word of God, 99
work tied to the word, 168

Scripture Index

Also Available in the Reformation Anglicanism Essential Library

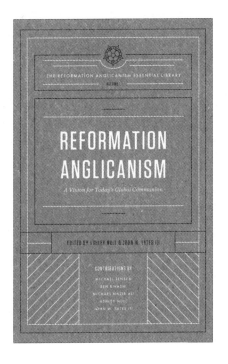

The Reformation Anglicanism Essential Library series sets out
to answer the question *What does it mean to be an Anglican today?*
Conceived with the conviction that the future of the
global Anglican Communion hinges on a clear, well-defined, and
theologically rich vision, each of the volumes in this set will introduce
a different aspect of the basic doctrinal and historical foundations
of the Anglican Communion rooted in the Reformation.

For more information, visit **crossway.org**.

A Catechism for Today's Increasingly Post-Christian World

"With Anglican churches filling with people who know little about orthodox and Anglican thought and practice, we need catechesis more than ever. This catechism will help our churches learn and walk in the beautiful Anglican way of living in the triune God."

GERALD R. MCDERMOTT, Former Anglican
Chair of Divinity, Beeson Divinity School

For more information, visit **crossway.org**.